THE GADGIL FORMULA

THE GADGIL FORMULA

For Allocation of
Central Assistance for State Plans

B.P.R. VITHAL
M.L. SASTRY

CENTRE FOR ECONOMIC AND SOCIAL STUDIES

MANOHAR
2002

First published 2002

ISBN 81-7304-479-1

Published by
Director
Centre for Economic and Social Studies
Nizamia Observatory Campus,
Begumpet, Hyderabad 500016
and
Ajay Kumar Jain for
Manohar Publishers & Distributors
4753/23 Ansari Road, Daryaganj
New Delhi 110002

Printed at
Lordson Publishers Pvt. Ltd.
Delhi 110002

To the Memory of
Professor D.R. Gadgil
On the occasion of his
Birth Centenary
1901–2001

Contents

Foreword

The provisions in our Constitution, which deal with the financial relations between the Union and the States are of special interest because of the unique balance between the powers of the Union and of the States on which these are based. In order to build an integrated national economy, free from internal tax barriers, the more important taxes were assigned to the Union. To periodically correct the consequent imbalance between the functions allocated to the States and the resources available to them a constitutional mechanism was provided through Finance Commission.

Soon after the Constitution came into effect, the country embarked on a national effort at planned development. For this purpose, a National Development Council (NDC) was set up which was not a constitutional body. The National Plan was to consist of a Central Plan and Plans of all the States. Given the inadequate powers of taxation allocated to the States, this process required further transfer of financial resources from the Union to the States in the shape of Central assistance for State Plans. It was possible to effect this transfer also through the constitutional provisions. Nevertheless, either deliberately or inadvertently, plan assistance was allocated to the States by the Planning Commission and kept out of the jurisdiction of the Finance Commissions. Consequently, there has been a lively debate in the country about the relative efficiency and equity of the two types of transfers, which have come to be known as statutory, and non-statutory.

Initially, the plan assistance for each was fixed entirely at the discretion of the Planning Commission. This was not necessarily arbitrary. Nevertheless, the States wanted this to be done in a transparent and objective manner. A formula, was, therefore, evolved and approved for this purpose by the NDC which is known as the

Gadgil Formula. Similar formulae have been evolved by the various Finance Commissions for the purpose of distributing the proceeds of the divisible pool of shareable Union taxes among the different States. Economists have analysed these various formulae, on the basis of their equity and efficiency. There is a crucial difference between the Gadgil Formula and the formulae adopted by the various Commissions. The recommendations of the Finance Commissions, based on their own formula, have been treated more or less as awards. The Gadgil Formula, on the other hand, had to be approved by a consensus among the top political leadership of the country represented in the NDC. This was possible only because of the moral and professional stature of Professor D.R. Gadgil, then Deputy Chairman, Planning Commission. It has, therefore, rightly come to be known as the Gadgil Formula.

The authors of this book, B.P.R. Vithal and M.L. Sastry, are uniquely placed to study these processes in all their aspects because of their long and special experience. B.P.R. Vithal had been the Planning Secretary, and subsequently also the Finance Secretary, of Andhra Pradesh for nearly two decades. He was a member of the Tenth Finance Commission. M.L. Sastry served in the Financial Resources Division of the Planning Commission and he was attached to one of the Finance Commissions. He subsequently moved to the Planning Department of the Government of Andhra Pradesh. Both of them were, thus, actively associated with this process. This is a case study of the evolution and working of the Gadgil Formula.

A study, by these authors, of the working of the Finance Commissions, which covers the entire field of statutory transfer of resources to the States, was published by the Oxford University Press in 2001 under the title *Fiscal Federalism in India*. They have now covered the non-statutory transfers to States under the Gadgil Formula in this book. By a happy coincidence, this study was completed in a year which happened to be the birth centenary of Professor D.R. Gadgil. The authors have, therefore, included a chapter on the life and work of Professor Gadgil, who was a great economist and a unique personality.

Both the authors have been associated with the CESS from its very inception. We are, therefore, happy to publish this volume under the aegis of the CESS.

Director S. MAHENDRA DEV
Centre for Economic and Social Studies
August 2002

Preface

The growing magnitude of Central transfers to States through non-statutory channels has been an important and controversial issue in any discussion of Centre-State financial relations in our country. Therefore, when we began our study of fiscal federalism in India, we initially divided it into two parts, one dealing with statutory transfers and the other with non-statutory transfers. All non-statutory transfers were taking place under Article 282. The debate was entirely about the intention of this Article and whether making such large transfers was an abuse, or at least, a misuse of Article 282. Nevertheless, it was strictly not non-statutory. Several Finance Commissions had dealt with this issue where they considered the scope of Article 275. Therefore, we had to deal with most of these issues in our first study (*Fiscal Federalism in India*, OUP, 2001).

The terms 'non-statutory' and 'discretionary' are often taken as if they were synonymous. This need not always be so. 'Statutory' transfers may be 'non-discretionary' in so far as the Union Government is concerned. But they also are the result of a discretion or judgement exercised by a Finance Commission. In the initial period, transfers for plan assistance were not fixed on the basis of any objective formula. They might not have been arbitrary or discriminatory but their basis was not transparent. The body dealing with them, the Planning Commission, was not a constitutional body. It was only a creature of the Union, even if its members were no less eminent than members of the Finance Commissions. Therefore, it was felt that, in the interest of better Centre-State understanding, plan transfers also should be regulated by an objective formula. It was against this background that the Gadgil Formula was evolved.

After this, the controversies have been about the schemes the Union Government has been devising to escape the Gadgil Formula—such as the Centrally Sponsored Schemes. We, therefore, found that a study of fiscal federalism in India should also analyse the evolution and subsequent implementation of the Gadgil Formula. Accordingly, we have devoted the second part of our study to this. It is our good fortune that the completion of our work has coincided with the Birth Centenary of Prof. Gadgil. We therefore, dedicate this study to his memory.

Hyderabad
March 2001

B.P.R. VITHAL
M.L. SASTRY

1

Inter-Governmental Financial Transfers: An Overview

We have dealt with this subject in our earlier book—*Fiscal Federalism in India* (OUP, 2001), with specific reference to the constitutional aspects and the role of the Finance Commission. The Finance Commission, as a statutory body is intended to address the in-built vertical imbalance in financial resources between the Centre and the States and the horizontal imbalance among the States, and recommend transfer of resources. Besides the Finance Commission, there are other channels also for transfer of resources from the Centre to the States. Planning Commission, constituted by an executive order in 1950, is an important channel for such transfers.

PLANNING COMMISSION

Unlike the Finance Commission, the Planning Commission is not a constitutional body. Even though the idea of planned economic development has a long history, i.e. from the early 1930s, a statutory body like the Finance Commission was not contemplated by the Constitution framers.

In 1934, M. Visveswarayya published a Ten Year Plan with the objective of doubling the National Income. In 1938, a conference of the Provincial Ministers of Industries held under the Chairmanship of the then Congress President, Sri Subhas Chandra Bose, recommended that a commission called the All India National Planning Commission should be appointed to formulate a comprehensive scheme of national planning for the achievement of industrialization. A National Planning Committee was then constituted with Jawaharlal Nehru as the Chairman and K.T. Shah as the General Secretary. The Committee appointed 29 sub-committees to study and report on different sectors of the economy and on certain special problems relating to national planning. Though the work of the Committee was interrupted with the outbreak of the Second World War and the arrest and imprisonment of its Chairman, a number of sub-committees prepared reports relating to their respective fields, some in 1939 and 1940 and others in 1945 and 1946.

'A Brief Memorandum Outlining a Plan of Economic Development for India' by eight prominent Indian industrialists, 'The Peoples Plan' by M.N. Roy, and 'The Gandhian Plan' by Shriman Narayan, aroused considerable interest at that time.

Another significant development during this period was the increasing awareness shown by the Government of India for preparation of plans for post-War reconstruction. Post-War Reconstruction Committees were appointed by both the Central Government and the Provincial Governments and plans were prepared under their auspices. Study reports were prepared regarding problems of development in different sectors—some of the more well-known being the Burns Memorandum on the Technological Possibilities of Agricultural Development, Reports of various Panels on Industrial Development, Report on the Location of Industries in India by the Economic Advisor to the Government of India, Report of the Bhore Committee on Medical and Health Programmes, Sargent Report on Education, etc. The Government of India had also created, in 1944, a Planning and Development Department for coordinating the work regarding post-War reconstruction.

An Advisory Planning Board was appointed in October 1946 (by the Interim Government under Jawaharlal Nehru), with K.C. Neogy as Chairman, for reviewing the work that had already been done in the field of planning and make recommendations for the future including the machinery for planning. The Board, in its report submitted in December 1946, recommended the appointment of a single, compact, and authoritative organization for the purpose of planning. The Board also suggested that the proposed Planning Commission should be mainly advisory in character, the final decisions resting with the Government. The Commission was to be a non-political body whose members would not change with changes in political fortunes. It was specifically recommended that a consultative body of 25 to 30 members, consisting of members of Planning Commission, representatives of the Provinces and States, and also representatives of agriculture, industry, commerce, labour, science, and other interests.

By the time the Report of the Advisory Planning Board was available (1947), political events such as attainment of independence and Partition of the country, and the aftermath of Partition were moving fast. No machinery for drawing up an overall plan for the country was created till about three years after the Report of the Advisory Planning Board.

The idea for a planning organization was gathering support. The All India Congress Committee had emphasized the importance of 'planned Central direction' in 1947. The Economic Programme Committee (of the AICC) under the Chairmanship of Jawaharlal Nehru recommended in 1948 that a permanent Central Planning Commission should be appointed. The Congress Working Committee, in a resolution passed in January 1950, recommended to the Government of India that a 'statutory' Planning Commission should be set up.

The Government's intention to establish a Planning Commission was announced in the President's Address to the Parliament at the end of January 1950. The President mentioned that the Planning Commission was to be established 'so that the best use can be made of such resources as we possess for the development of the nation'. The actual announcement of the Commission was made by the Union Finance Minister in his Budget speech on 28 February 1950.

The Planning Commission was established by a Resolution of the Government of India dated 15 March 1950. 'For some years past', the Resolution stated, 'the people of India have been conscious of the importance of planned development as a means of raising the country's standard of living.' 'During the last three years', the Resolution further added, 'the Centre as well as the Provinces have initiated schemes of development but experience has shown that progress has been hampered by the absence of adequate co-ordination and of sufficiently precise information about the availability of resources.' As a result of various problems that the country was facing, 'the need for comprehensive planning based on a careful appraisal of resources and on an objective analysis of all relevant economic factors has become imperative. These purposes can best be achieved through an organization free from the burden of the day-to-day administration, but in constant touch with the Government at the highest policy level.'

The Resolution referred to the Constitution of India, and especially to certain Directive Principles of State Policy, and stated that in view of these and the 'declared objective of the Government to promote a rapid rise in the standard of living of the people', a Planning Commission was being set up with the following functions:

(1) make an assessment of the material, capital, and human resources of the country, including technical personnel and investigate the possibilities of augmenting such of these resources as are found to be deficient in relation to the nation's requirements;
(2) formulate a plan for the most effective and balanced utilization of the country's resources;
(3) on a determination of the priorities, define the stages in which the plan should be carried out and propose the allocation of resources for the due completion of each stage;
(4) indicate the factors which are tending to retard economic development and determine the conditions which, in view of the current social and political situation, should be established for the successful execution of the plan;
(5) determine the nature of the machinery which will be necessary for securing the successful implementation of each stage of the plan in all its aspects;
(6) appraise, from time to time, the progress achieved in the execution of each stage of the plan and recommend the adjustments of policy and measures that such appraisal may show to be necessary; and
(7) make such interim or ancillary recommendations as appear to be appropriate either for facilitating the discharge of the duties assigned to it or on a consideration of the prevailing economic conditions, current policies, measures and development programmes, or on an examination of such specific problems as may be referred to it for advice by Central or State Governments.

The Resolution indicated that the Commission would be essentially an advisory body and would make recommendations to the Cabinet. 'In framing its recommendations', the Resolution stated, 'the Commission will act in close understanding and consultation with the Ministries of the Central Government and the Governments of the States.' The Resolution expressed confidence that the States would give the fullest measure of help to the Commission so as to ensure the maximum coordination in policy and unity in effort. It stressed the importance of the work of the Commission for the future welfare of the people in every sphere of national life and emphasized that its success would depend on the extent to which it enlisted the association and cooperation of the people at all levels. The Government expressed the hope that in carrying out this task, the Commission would receive the maximum support and goodwill from all interests and, in particular, from industry and labour. The full text of this Resolution is given in Appendix I.

Table 1.1 gives an idea of the transfer of resources from the Centre to the States, from the Finance Commission and the Planning Commission from 1951 to 1997. (They exclude other discretionary transfers from various Central Ministries.)

TABLE 1.1: TRANSFER OF RESOURCES FROM THE CENTRE TO THE STATES

Period	F.C.	P.C.	Total	F.C.	P.C.	Total
	(Rs. crores)			Percentages		
First Plan 1951–6	447	880	1,327	33.7	66.3	100
Second Plan 1956–61	918	1,058	1,936	47.4	52.6	100
Third Plan 1961–6	1,590	2,738	4,328	36.7	63.3	100
Ann. Plans 1966–9	1,782	1,917	3,699	48.2	51.8	100
Fourth Plan 1969–74	5,421	4,731	10,152	53.4	46.6	100
Fifth Plan 1974–8	8,395	6,537	14,932	56.2	44.8	100
Ann. Plans 1978–80	6,142	6,603	12,745	48.2	51.8	100
Sixth Plan 1980–5	24,998	25,747	50,745	49.3	50.7	100
Seventh Plan 1985–90	54,388	54,308	1,08,696	50.0	50.0	100
Ann. Plans 1990–2	35,437	33,677	69,114	51.3	48.7	100
Eighth Plan 1992–7	1,45,341	1,31,213	2,76,554	52.6	47.4	100

Source: First Plan to Fourth Plan—as given in the Report of the Seventh Finance Commission. Fifth Plan to Eighth Plan—as given in RBI Bulletins.

It will be seen that transfers from the Planning Commission for State Plans, Centrally Sponsored Schemes, and Central sector plans, occupied a very important place in the scheme of financial transfers from the Centre to the States. Broadly speaking, the Finance Commission deals with the non-plan revenue account position of States; and the Planning Commission deals with the developmental needs of the States covering both revenue and capital accounts. Both these Commissions work in the background of the constitutionally in-built vertical imbalance between the Centre and the States. As far as the horizontal imbalance among the States is concerned, their respective roles are somewhat different. Within the constraint of the overall amount that they can transfer to the States, the Finance Commission has a free hand to evolve its distribution formula. Planning Commission, however, has to work under the overall directions of the National Development Council, which has to arrive at its decisions through discussion and consensus.

2

Background to the Gadgil Formula

POST-WAR DEVELOPMENT SCHEMES

The practice of providing Central assistance to States for financing their development programmes and schemes was in vogue even before the advent of Five Year Plans in 1951. On the termination of World War II, the Central and Provincial Governments had embarked upon certain development projects and the Provinces received assistance from the Centre in the form of grants under, what were then known as, Post-War Reconstruction and Development Grants. Though some of these grants were done away with by 1951, those for Grow More Food Schemes and certain other special schemes continued. These grants were being given, initially, under Section 150(2) of the Government of India Act, 1935 and under Article 282 of the Constitution of India, after its adoption in 1950.

FIRST FIVE YEAR PLAN: 1951–1956

The First Five Year Plan 1951-6 of the States comprised some of the Post-War Reconstruction and Development Schemes, which were already in progress in the States and some new additional schemes and programmes. In the total Five Year Plan outlay originally estimated at Rs. 2,069 crores, the outlay of Part 'A' and Part 'B' States accounted for Rs. 800 crores. Many schemes, which should have appropriately been included in the State Sector, were included in the Central Sector, as the exact distribution of their financial liability had not been decided upon by then. Multipurpose River Valley Schemes like Damodar Valley, Bhakhra-Nangal, Hirakund, and Harike; Community Development Projects; Projects for Special Minor Irrigation; Local Works; Projects for Scarcity Affected Areas;

Basic and Social Education; Industrial Housing, etc., came under this category.

Originally, a Central assistance of Rs. 193 crores for the Plan outlay of Rs. 800 crores in the State Sector, was communicated to the States. The actual expenditure on the States' First Five Year Plan amounted to Rs. 879 crores. The actual Central assistance released for the State plan schemes amounted to Rs. 332 crores. For the schemes mentioned earlier, which were included in the Central Sector, an amount of Rs. 548 crores was distributed among the States.

No clear indication was available as to how the allocation of Central assistance to States was decided upon for the First Five Year Plan. One can only infer that a judgement was exercised, keeping in view the priorities and requirements of the various schemes and availability of resources for the same. Even though the amount of assistance was arrived at after discussions with the Chief Ministers regarding the resources of the States and the nature of the projects in the Plan (i.e. continuing irrigation and power projects and the programmes relating to agricultural production, etc.), the position remained fluid for a variety of reasons. Firstly, the Plan itself was finalized a year after the programmes had been taken up for implementation on the basis of 'The Outline'. Secondly, the First Finance Commission's recommendations became available only in December 1952. In the circumstances, the position regarding normal devolution of funds between the Centre and the States could not be clearly visualized at the time of Plan formulation in 1950. The following extracts from the First Five Year Plan Document are relevant in this connection:

> Over the period of the Plan there will be a flow of assistance from the Centre to the States under a variety of heads. Apart from grants-in-aid of a statutory nature, the States will receive assistance in the form of loans for river valley schemes, minor irrigation, rehabilitation of displaced persons, community development projects, cottage and small industries, and other schemes of development included in the Plan as well as grants from the Central Road Fund for construction of roads, grants for relief of displaced persons, grants for raising food production, etc. For operational reasons many of the schemes of development, for which the assistance mentioned

above will be given, are included in the Plan as part of the development schemes of the Central Government and so the estimated assistance for the State Plans as such works out to only about Rs. 193 crores. But this, we must emphasise, is only a matter of presentation and the share of the States in the development programme of the Public Sector, as well as the magnitude of the transfers, which will be necessary from the Centre to the States, are both very much larger than would appear at first sight.

In the 'Central assistance' as estimated for operational purposes referred to above, has been included assistance only under the following heads: bonuses on food procurement (now discontinued), grants and loans for Grow More Food Campaign, special grants for Part 'B' States for development, and loans for Miscellaneous Development Schemes.

From a preliminary review of the working of the State Plan schemes in 1952, and the budgets of State Governments for 1952–53, it would appear that the task of organising finances to the pattern outlined in the above paragraphs has, by and large, yet to begin. These considerations as well as the relative merits of the schemes, which are now being added on as compared to the schemes, which were originally in the State Plans, are matters, which deserve close examination. But we must emphasise that the capacity of the Centre to give additional assistance is limited. The whole scheme of Central assistance as now worked out may have also to be readjusted in the light of the recommendations of the First Finance Commission. All these would have to form part of the reassessment of State finances referred to already.

SECOND FIVE YEAR PLAN: 1956–1961

At the commencement of the Second Five Year plan a majority of the schemes, which were included in the Central sector during the First Plan but were being implemented by the States outside their Plans, were transferred to the State Sector and included in the State Plans.

The Plan outlays of individual States were decided after discussions between the Planning Commission and the State Chief Ministers. The considerations which the Planning Commission had kept in view in determining the size of the individual State Plans were set out in a Paper presented to the National Development Council (NDC) in September 1955, as under:

In considering the magnitude of the Plan of a State for the period 1956–61, the Planning commission has taken into account a number of factors. No single criterion or formula, if applied by itself in a uniform manner to all States, is found to be adequate or tenable. The principal considerations are:

(i) Population;
(ii) Commitments carried over from the First Plan to the Second Plan with reference to irrigation and power projects as well as other heads of development;
(iii) The extent of development during the First Five Year Plan and the general level of development expected to be reached at the end of the First Plan;
(iv) The revenue position of a State as represented both by its total revenue and the extent to which it is able to finance its Second Plan on the revenue account; and
(v) The programme of irrigation and power projects for the Second Plan, especially in the light of the examination and recommendations of the Technical Committee for Irrigation and Power.

The resources of all the States taken together amounted to approximately Rs. 826 crores against the outlay of Rs. 2,103 crores, thus leaving a gap of Rs. 1,277 crores. The quantum of Central assistance for each State had not been indicated but it was mentioned in the Plan Document that in view of the fact that resources of all the States taken together fell short of the requirements by as much as 60 per cent, large transfers of resources from the Centre to the States were inevitable. The Central assistance on account of Annual Plan outlay was accordingly settled each year after discussions. As against the gap of Rs. 1,277 crores in resources, the Central assistance actually given to the States during the Second Five Year Plan period amounted to Rs.1,058 crores.

THIRD FIVE YEAR PLAN: 1961–1966

The outlays as well as the quantum of Central assistance for the Third Five Year Plan for each State were decided after discussions with the State Chief Ministers. Considerations which governed the determination of outlays of the States for the Third Plan were indicated in a Paper of the Planning Commission placed before the NDC at its sixteenth meeting held on 12 and 13 September 1960. They were summarized in the Third Five Year Plan Document:

> In determining the Plan of each State, consideration was given to its needs, problems, past progress and the lags in development, likely contribution to the achievement of major national targets, potential for growth and the contribution in resources which the State could make towards its development programmes. In assessing needs and problems, such factors as population, area, levels of income and expenditure, commitments carried over from the Second Plan, commitments on account of large projects or special programmes and the state of technical and administrative services available, were taken into account. Care was also taken to see that States, whose resources were unavoidably small, did not have to limit development to a scale, which was altogether insufficient, merely because of paucity of resources. At the same time, States, which were able to make a larger effort in mobilising their own resources, could undertake development on an appropriate scale.

The States' resources for the Third Five Year Plan were estimated at Rs. 1,462 crores and Central assistance at Rs. 2,375 crores. Intimation about Central assistance allocated for individual States was given to the State Governments before the commencement of the Plan. Central assistance for the Annual Plan was decided after discussions with each State after examination of its resources and the requirement of the Plan programmes.

It may be observed here that during the first three Five Year Plans, stress was laid mainly on the principles, which would determine the Plan outlays rather than the quantum of Central assistance. Central assistance was largely decided in the light of the gap in resources of individual States in relation to the Plan outlays decided upon. Amounts of assistance for the Annual Plans were invariably decided upon at the time of Annual Plan discussions.

FOURTH FIVE YEAR PLAN: 1966–1971

After fifteen years of centralized planning and the exercise of discretionary powers by the Planning Commission in deciding upon the overall plan outlays through the allocation of Central assistance, the States were chafing at the bit and were demanding the evolution of objective criteria for allocation of Central assistance and simplification of the channelling of such assistance. The desirability of evolving objective criteria for allocation of Central assistance was emphasized by several Chief Ministers during discussions on the Preliminary Memorandum on the Fourth Five Year Plan 1966–71, held in June–July 1965. Views of the State Governments on this subject were, thereupon, invited and incorporated in a paper placed before the NDC in August 1966. The Chief Ministers expressed divergent views suggesting different criteria, depending on their own priorities and circumstances, which would give them relative advantage as compared to other possible alternatives. No agreed conclusions, therefore, could be reached in the NDC, which asked the Planning Commission to evolve a set of principles in the light of discussions held in the NDC. Accordingly, the Planning Commission drew up the following guidelines for determining the quantum of Central assistance for each State for the period of the Fourth Five Year Plan 1966–71, as then envisaged.

(i) Every State should first receive 70 per cent of the total amount to be distributed as Central assistance, in proportion to its population;

(ii) The balance should be distributed after taking into account:

  (a) Special needs of the States of Assam, Jammu & Kashmir, and Nagaland;

  (b) Commitments of some of the States required to incur large outlays on continuing irrigation and power schemes which are of national importance; and

  (c) The requirements for ensuring accelerated development of certain backward regions, hill areas, etc.

For financing States' Plan outlay of Rs. 7,073 crores indicated in the Draft Outline of the Fourth Five Year Plan 1966–71 (August 1966), Central assistance was envisaged at Rs. 3,500 crores. On the basis of the guidelines mentioned earlier, the Planning Commission finalized the amounts of Central assistance and Plan outlays after detailed discussions with the State Chief Ministers in October 1966. The total assistance indicated to the States in these discussions aggregated to Rs. 3,571 crores. However, finalization of the Fourth Five Year Plan was postponed due to the war with Pakistan and its effect on the economy in the aftermath. This resulted in three successive Annual Plans of 1966–7, 1967–8 and 1968–9. The Fourth Five Year Plan actually commenced from 1969–70.

The Annual Plan for the year 1966–7 had to be finalized before the conclusion of discussions with the States on their Five Year Plans, and the amounts of Central assistance for that year had to be intimated in time for their budgets. Certain States had to be given accelerated assistance to meet the situation created by external aggression, drought conditions and commitments on account of continuing schemes. The quantum of assistance for the Annual Plan of 1966–7 was, therefore, decided on an *ad hoc* basis. An indication was, however, given to the State Chief Ministers that amounts so given would be adjusted later in the overall assistance decided for the Five Year Plan.

The Annual Plan for 1967–8 had to be formulated in very difficult circumstances when the resources at the disposal of the Centre were extremely limited and the drought conditions continued in several parts of the country. The commitments of some of the States in respect of continuing schemes necessitated allocation of accelerated assistance to them. As a result, the distribution of Central assistance had to be on an *ad hoc* basis again.

It was decided by the Central Government to treat the Plan outlays for the three years—1966–7, 1967–8 and 1968–9 as Annual Plans and formulate a new Fourth Five Year Plan for the period 1969–74.

Prof. D.R. Gadgil, the then Director of the Gokhale Institute of Politics and Economics, Poona, was appointed as Deputy Chairman of the Planning Commission on 1 September 1967, with the task of formulation of a new Fourth Five Year Plan for 1969–74.

The effect of *ad hoc* distribution of Central assistance over the years 1966–7 and 1967–8 was to deprive some States of their legitimate share in Central assistance. These States were pressing for making up the entire shortfall (over these two years), during the year 1968–9 itself. Notionally, all the States had to be given the agreed assistance over a period of five years. The excess or shortfall in Central assistance given during these two years, as compared to the legitimate entitlements on a proportionate basis, was decided to be adjusted equally over the remaining three years and the first such adjustment was made in 1968–9.

Considering the fact that a new Five Year Plan for 1969–74 was being contemplated, the Planning Commission felt that it would be appropriate to re-examine the principles underlying the distribution of Central assistance to States. The Commission asked the State Governments to formulate their views in this regard and the points that emerged from these views are:

(i) A few States suggested that a major portion of the total Central assistance should be distributed on the basis of *population*. Kerala: 50 per cent; Gujarat: 60 per cent; Haryana: 70 per cent; Bihar, Uttar Pradesh and Maharashtra: 80 per cent; West Bengal: 90 to 100 per cent. The Governments of Punjab and Rajasthan were opposed to population being the main criterion for the distribution of Central assistance.

(ii) West Bengal, Kerala, and Uttar Pradesh suggested that special consideration should be given to the requirements of *border States* of Jammu & Kashmir, Assam, and Nagaland; and *hill areas and especially backward areas* in different States.

(iii) Andhra Pradesh, Kerala, Punjab, and Rajasthan were of the view that the Plan outlay should be determined first on the basis of needs, problems, resource potential, etc., of each State. The quantum of Central assistance should be determined on the basis of *the essential plan outlay and the resources of the State.*

(iv) Haryana, Madhya Pradesh, Punjab, Uttar Pradesh, and Rajasthan laid stress on meeting *the full requirements of large, continuing irrigation and power projects.*

(v) Andhra Pradesh, Punjab, Haryana, and Kerala suggested that *investments of the Central Sector Plan within the State boundaries* should be taken into consideration in deciding upon the quantum of assistance for individual States.

(vi) Kerala suggested that the *food deficit* of a State and the vulnerability of its economy to *fluctuations in the export market* should be taken into consideration.

(vii) West Bengal suggested that the *revenue surplus* on account of the recommendations of the Finance Commission should be taken into account in finalizing Central assistance. But Maharashtra was opposed to this approach.

(viii) Orissa suggested fixation of Central assistance for each State after *mutual discussions* and not on the basis of *any predetermined criteria* and also after the recommendations of the Fifth Finance Commission are available.

(ix) Madras suggested that *pressure of population* as well as certain special factors such as *influx of repatriates from abroad*, should be the criteria for distribution of Central assistance among States and that the criterion of relative backwardness of States does not ensure objectivity due to lack of comparable indicators of development.

On the basis of the views expressed by different States, the Planning Commission posed the following issues for the consideration of the National Development Council.

1. Should the Central assistance for individual States be predetermined for the Plan period as a whole? Should the allocations in the Annual Plan of a State be necessarily in proportion to the predetermined five year assistance? If not, what should be the considerations governing the variations from year to year? How should adjustments be made to ensure correspondence with the predetermined assistance for the five years?
2. If the assistance for individual States is not predetermined for a five year period, what should be the principles governing the distribution of Annual Plan assistance?
3. Should special consideration be given to the requirements of border States like Jammu & Kashmir, Assam, and Nagaland as hitherto?
4. Should population constitute one of the main criteria for determining Central assistance, and if so, what should be the weight given to it?
5. What weights should be given to the following factors in determining the quantum of assistance to individual States?

(a) Economic backwardness of a State as determined by per capita income, concentration of tribal population, markedly backward and hill areas, chronically drought affected and desert areas.
(b) Commitments on account of continuing schemes.
(c) Potential for raising resources and the performance of individual States in mobilizing them.
(d) Central Sector investments in individual States.
(e) The quantum of assistance received by each State over the previous 18 years.
(f) Special features such as density of population, rehabilitation of displaced persons, etc.

The twenty-fifth meeting of the National Development Council was held on 17 and 18 May 1968. The Agenda Papers for this meeting included:

I. Approach to the Fourth Five Year Plan
II. Principles for the Distribution of Central Assistance
III. Patterns of Central Assistance
IV. Recommendations of the Administrative Reforms Commission on the Machinery for Planning

Prime Minister, Indira Gandhi welcomed the State Chief Ministers and other Members and briefly explained the purpose of the crucial meeting which was to mainly 'consider the basic approach to the Fourth Plan, the overall goals, the tempo and pattern of development, the national effort, the discipline, cooperation and determination required for reaching the set goals'. The Prime Minister then requested the Deputy Chairman, Planning Commission to explain in greater detail some of the underlying assumptions and problems inherent in the approach to the Fourth Plan. Summary Record of this meeting stated, *inter alia,*

110. On the other two items relating to (1) Principles for the distribution of Central assistance and (2) Patterns of Central assistance for Centrally Aided and Centrally Sponsored Schemes, which had been placed before the National Development Council for consideration, it was decided that a Committee of all State Chief Ministers with the Deputy Chairman, Planning

Commission as the Chairman should be set up which should go into these. It was also agreed that the Union Ministers concerned should be associated when the Centrally aided/sponsored schemes relating to their sectors were taken up for consideration by the Committee.

The NDC Committee met twice, in July and September 1968, to discuss these issues. During the deliberations of the Committee, the Chief Ministers of States expressed divergent views, firstly regarding the criteria and secondly about the weights to be allotted to different criteria. The Chief Ministers of Andhra Pradesh, Assam, Kerala, and Rajasthan emphasized that the existing imbalances in the economic development of different States should be taken into consideration and States which did not receive adequate share of Central investment in the past should be given higher Central assistance as a compensatory factor so as to accelerate the rate of investment in the Fourth Plan period. After some discussion it was decided that the question of imbalances be considered as a separate item on the agenda.

There was considerable difference of opinion in the matter of weights to be assigned to the population criterion. Chief Ministers of States like Uttar Pradesh, Bihar, West Bengal, and Madras (Tamil Nadu) wanted 80 to 90 per cent of the divisible pool of Central assistance to be distributed among the States on the basis of population. On the other hand, Chief Ministers of States like Haryana, Kerala, Mysore (Karnataka), Punjab, and Rajasthan wanted that the weight for population criterion should not be more than 50 per cent. After detailed discussions, it was unanimously decided that the population criterion be assigned a weight of 60 per cent.

After the Committee had agreed to per capita income as one of the criteria, the question arose whether Central assistance on the basis of this criterion should be given to all the States or restricted to only those States whose per capita income was below the national average. According to the then available statistics of per capita income, six out of the total fourteen non-special category States, namely, Bihar, Kerala, Madhya Pradesh, Orissa, Rajasthan, and Uttar Pradesh had per capita income below the national average. The Committee decided to restrict assistance under this criterion to the States having per capita income below the national average only and also decided that the per capita income figures to be used for this purpose, should be agreed figures and taken as an average of three consecutive years. The discussion then centred on the methods of calculation, i.e. distance method v.s. deviation method. It was not realized by all for some time that the distance method was linked to all States having a share under this criterion also, while the deviation method would take the all-States average as the basis and only States with a per capita income below the average would be entitled for assistance under this criterion. (It may be mentioned in passing that, this confusion also arose at the time of the second modification of the Gadgil Formula in 1991. Sri Pranab Mukherjee first proposed that the weight for this criterion be increased by 10 percentage points and that the entire 30 per cent be on the basis of the distance method, implying that all States would be entitled under this criterion (see Chapter 7.) When this implication was realized, the Chief Minister of Kerala stated that all States were getting a share under all other criteria, which would not be necessarily weighted by the backwardness of the States. These criteria like tax effort and spill-over commitments were such that they would benefit the advanced States more. Therefore, at least this small percentage of 10 should be left for backward States only. There was a stalemate on this point and an appeal was made to the Deputy Chairman to suggest a way out. Prof. Gadgil said that 'the formula had to be evolved by a consensus. The Planning Commission had suggested certain broad criteria. But on an issue such as this one, the consensus had to evolve from amongst the Chief Ministers and he would not like to intervene.' At this stage, the meeting was adjourned.

After the meeting Sri K. Brahmananda Reddy, Chief Minister of Andhra Pradesh discussed this issue with Sri Sukhadia, Chief Minister of Rajasthan. They felt that leaving 10 per cent for backward States alone, would only be fair especially when it included the two populous States of Bihar and Uttar Pradesh. They, therefore, went to Sri V.P. Naik, Chief Minister of Maharashtra and explained this rationale to him. They argued that if Sri Naik took the initiative and agreed on behalf of the most advanced State (at that time), every one else would agree. Sri Naik agreed and, accordingly, when the

Committee reconvened next day, Sri Naik intervened and said that Maharashtra was agreeable to the suggestion made by the Chief Minister of Kerala. The other Chief Ministers, who had not been a party to the previous evening's discussion, were all pleasantly surprised and readily agreed.*

The Committee thus resolved that 10 per cent of the divisible pool of Central assistance should be distributed only to those States whose per capita income is below the national average. The Committee also decided on three other criteria, viz., tax effort, continuing major irrigation and power projects, and special problems of States with a weight of 10 per cent each.

At its final meeting held on 13 September 1968, the Committee unanimously adopted a formula, which formed the basis for distribution of Central assistance for the Fourth Five Year Plan period. This formula, suggested by the NDC Committee, was considered

* Personal recollections of Sri B.P.R. Vithal.

I accompanied Sri Brahmananda Reddy, Chief Minister of Andhra Pradesh to the meetings of the NDC Committee as Secretary (Planning), Government of Andhra Pradesh. This is based on my recollection of that meeting. As we were coming out of the first day's meeting, Sri Brahmananda Reddy asked me for my opinion on this item. I told him that I had figures of per capita income of Andhra Pradesh only for one year as prepared by the State Bureau of Economics and Statistics. According to this, Andhra Pradesh was below the national average. But, I said, that irrespective of this consideration my own view was that the Chief Minister of Kerala had a valid point. At least 10 per cent should be left for distribution to the backward States alone. Sri Brahmananda Reddy agreed and discussed it with Sri Sukhadia first, while I was present. Then the two went to Sri Naik's residence. Sri Brahmananda Reddy informed me that Sri Naik had also agreed.

On the basis of the CSO's methodology and three years' average, Andhra Pradesh was then not below the national average. But Sri Brahmananda Reddy did not mind this. There was a separate instance in another context when the State Bureau's estimate of surplus rice in A.P. proved to be wrong and embarassed the Government. On that issue, Sri Brahmananda Reddy took the Director of the Bureau to task. Mr. Daniel Thorner made an issue out of this in the *Economic and Political Weekly*, in those days. In my view, Sri Brahmananda Reddy was right on that issue. But on this issue, i.e. the per capita income of Andhra Pradesh, Sri Brahmananda Reddy did not say anything; nor, in my view, was his stand in the NDC Committee based on the narrow consideration of A.P's own position under this criterion.

by the twenty-sixth meeting of the National Development Council held on 19 and 20 April 1969.

The National Development Council adopted the recommendations of the 'Committee of the NDC', and asked the Planning Commission to work out the final distribution of Central assistance on the basis of the objective criteria approved by it. It is this formula that has come to be known as *The Gadgil Formula*. The Gadgil Formula approved by the NDC covered (a) distribution criteria, (b) patterns of assistance, (c) channelling of assistance, and (d) Centrally Sponsored Schemes. For the sake of convenience, we have dealt with these aspects in separate chapters.

3

The Gadgil Formula

The unanimous recommendations made by the NDC Committee (referred to in the previous chapter) and approved by the National Development Council in its meeting held in April 1969 covered, as stated in the previous chapter, a formula for the distribution of Central assistance for State Plans, patterns of assistance, procedure for channelling of assistance, and the quantum of outlays on Centrally Sponsored Schemes. We are dealing with the formula for distribution of Central assistance in this chapter.

Briefly stated, the original Gadgil Formula for distribution of Central assistance for State Plans was as follows:

1. The requirements of the States of Assam, Jammu & Kashmir, and Nagaland should first be met out of the total pool of Central assistance.
2. The balance of the Central assistance should then be distributed among the remaining fourteen States on the basis of the following criteria:

   (i) 60 per cent on the basis of population;
   (ii) 10 per cent on the basis of per capita state income—only to those States whose per capita income is below the national average;
   (iii) 10 per cent on the basis of tax effort of individual States, determined on the basis of 'State's per capita tax receipts as percentage of State's per capita income';
   (iv) 10 per cent on the basis of spill over outlay into the Fourth Plan, of major continuing irrigation and power schemes; and
   (v) 10 per cent for special problems of individual States; special problems indicated by the NDC Committee being—existence of border areas in a State, desert areas, flood affected

areas, chronically drought affected areas, metropolitan areas, existence of untapped resources, population of displaced persons or refugees, and percentage of unemployed in the total population.

In this connection, the following extracts from the speech of Prof. Gadgil, Deputy Chairman, Planning Commission, at the meeting of the NDC held on 19 April 1969, are illuminating.

9. Deputy Chairman stated that since the report of the Fifth Finance Commission was still awaited, a clear picture of Centre's own liabilities was not available, but notwithstanding this the Central Government had agreed, on the recommendations of the Planning Commission, to keep their contribution to the State plans at Rs. 3,500 crores.

10. Deputy Chairman referred to the principles for the distribution of Central assistance to States which had been evolved at the meeting of the NDC Committee of State Chief Ministers held in September 1968. It was agreed that the requirements of the States of Assam, Jammu & Kashmir and Nagaland be met through an *ad hoc* lump assignment out of the total Central assistance, and that the balance should be distributed as follows: 60 per cent on the basis of population, 10 per cent on the basis of per capita income only to the States below the national average, 10 per cent on the basis of tax effort in relation to per capita income, 10 per cent on account of continuing major irrigation and power schemes and the remaining 10 per cent on consideration of special problems of States.

11. Indicating the guidelines adopted by the Planning Commission in distributing Central assistance in accordance with the above criteria, Deputy Chairman stated:

Population: population figures for 1 October 1966, supplied by the Registrar General, had been taken as the base.

Per Capita Income: As regards the per capita income, the comparable estimates of income, prepared by the Central Statistical Organization for different States on a uniform basis for the average of the three latest consecutive years for which such estimates were available, viz., 1962–3, 1963–4 and 1964–5, had been taken as the basis. Assistance under this head had been distributed to the States of Bihar, Kerala, Madhya Pradesh, Orissa, Rajasthan and Uttar Pradesh, whose per capita income was below the national average according to the CSO estimates. Central assistance had been distributed among them on the 'deviation method'. This would provide assistance to the weaker States with due weightage to population and was considered more equitable than the 'inverse ratio method' recommended by some States.

Tax Effort: For the tax effort, the distribution was to be based on the tax effort in relation to the per capita income. For the latter, the CSO figures for 1962–3 to 1964–5 had been taken. For tax receipts, the data for 1967–8 had been adopted as indicated by the NDC Committee. Only State taxes had been taken into consideration and not the States' share of Central taxes. The ratio of tax receipts to State's income was worked out and thereafter the distribution was made on the 'direct proportion' method.

[One State suggested that the ratio of tax effort should be worked out after taking out from the State income the amount of Central taxes collected within the territory of the State and the outflow of income from the State. Some States suggested the adoption of the 'deviation method' instead of the 'direct proportion method'. Both these were considered. As regards the first, since it is the income before tax which is the index of the ability to pay and not the income after the tax; and also the estimates of State income are based on the 'income originating' concept rather than the 'income accrual' concept, these suggestions could not be accepted. Moreover, there are no reliable data and method available to estimate outflows of income from a State. As regards the second, the Commission came to the conclusion that in adopting the 'deviation method', population will get an added weight which would not be justified and several of the smaller States which have considerable tax effort to their credit will stand to loose substantially. On the other hand, States with large population would gain unduly even though their tax effort may be substantially below the all-India average. The Commission, therefore, adopted the 'direct proportion method'.]

Spill-over Commitments: The 10 per cent on account of continuing major irrigation and power schemes had been determined in relation to major schemes whose total project cost was estimated at more than Rs. 20 crores and in whose case it was expected that the expenditure up to the end of 1968-9 would be, at least, 10 per cent of the estimated project cost. Since actual expenditure for 1968–9 was not available, and would not be available till September/October 1969, this had been interpreted to mean the actual expenditure up to the end of 1967–8 plus the outlay approved by the

Commission for the Annual Plan 1968–9. In regard to the total cost of the project, the estimates approved by the Planning Commission for expenditure on particular projects during the Fourth Plan had been taken into account. The assistance of Rs. 310 crores had been distributed among the various States in a fixed proportion which had been worked out on the basis of the amount to be distributed among the States (Rs. 310 crores) in relation to the total outlay envisaged in the Fourth Plan for all these projects. (Rs. 915 crores)

Special Problems: In respect of the last 10 per cent, the Commission had taken into consideration the various major problems of the individual States. They have taken note of the identifiable and integrated plans of development prepared by the States for problems such as those for chronically drought affected areas, desert areas, hill areas, tribal areas, metropolitan areas and flood affected areas. Taking various aspects into account such as the expected outlay in relation to these problems during the Fourth Plan and the resources position of each State, the Commission applied their best judgement in distributing the last Rs. 310 crores among the different States.

12. Deputy Chairman also referred to the decision taken by the NDC Committee of State Chief Ministers to abolish different patterns of assistance attached to specific schemes and stated that the total assistance would now be divided among block loans and grants. The matching element in Centrally Sponsored Schemes had also been abolished and these would now be on a hundred per cent assistance basis. The number of Centrally Sponsored Schemes had also been considerably reduced.

13. Determination of the distribution of Central assistance to States according to fixed criteria and the abolition of different patterns of assistance attached to specific schemes had made for a very large degree of freedom for State effort in planning. The size of Plans of individual States in the Fourth Plan and for the Annual Plans would be determined by Central assistance and the resources that the State was willing and able to raise. As regards the Union Territories, their Plan outlays were entirely dependent on Central allocations. These outlays had been maintained at about the level proposed in the earlier Draft Outline of the Fourth Plan (1966–71)

In the earlier plan periods, the Planning Commission was determining the total plan outlay necessary for a State and the resources the State could reasonably be expected to rise as per agreed estimates after a discussion with the Planning Commission, and the Central assistance necessary was derived as the difference between these two parameters. There was a feeling among the States that this process was not objective enough, and it is this feeling that gave rise to the demand for an objective formula for the distribution of Central assistance. The Gadgil Formula was adopted as an attempt to bring about an objectivity in the distribution of Central assistance.

But in this new dispensation, the total outlay on the State Plan became, automatically, the sum total of the State's own resources and the Central assistance, determined on the basis of the Gadgil Formula. There was no scope for discretion or any special consideration as regards Central assistance. This period coincided with a decline in the total Central assistance available for State plans. At the same time, the buoyancy of some of the State taxes, such as sales tax, entertainment tax, and motor vehicles tax went up. The result was that, in the case of more prosperous States, the State's own resources was a larger component than Central assistance. Meanwhile, the share of market borrowings in plan financing also went up. The total market borrowings as well as the market borrowing to each State is determined at the time of finalization of the State plans after discussions between the Reserve Bank, the Government of India, Finance Ministry, and the Planning Commission. For a long time the market borrowing by each State was fixed as a percentage increase over the previous year's borrowing. This also favoured the more prosperous States. Thus, out of the three factors which determined the total plan outlay of a State, two, viz., the State's own resources and market borrowings, were going up autonomously, while the objective and equitable Gadgil Formula determined only one factor, viz., Central Plan assistance. Thus, the prosperous States continued to have large Plan outlays in spite of the Gadgil Formula.

This Formula was in operation for the Fourth Five Year Plan, 1969–74.

4

Patterns and Channelling of Central Assistance

Until the end of the First Five Year Plan, Central assistance was given to the States for various schemes formulated by the different Ministries irrespective of whether or not those schemes were included in the States' Plans. All such development schemes, which were not included in the States' First Five Year Plans, were transferred to the State Sector with the commencement of the Second Five Year Plan. Different conditions such as the loan-grant mix for various components of a single scheme were attached to schemes controlled by different Ministries. The patterns of assistance, which applied to the schemes under various sectors, were adopted by the Planning Commission without any change for channelling Central assistance to States during the Second Plan period. The large number of varying conditions attached to individual schemes rendered the calculation of entitlement of assistance and release of the same rather cumbersome and difficult.

In all, there were 185 State Plan schemes carrying different patterns of assistance at that time. The largest number (100) was under Agricultural Programmes, followed by General and Technical Education (23), Cooperation (20), Industry (18), Health (15), and so on. States found it extremely difficult to make an estimation of assistance under loans and grants for the schemes based on the bewildering number of patterns. The settlement of accounts and adjustments in Central assistance also became complicated.

The position was reviewed at the end of the Second Five Year Plan with a view to rationalize and reduce the number of patterns in consultation with the State Governments and Central Ministries. The number of schemes, to which patterns were applicable, was reduced to 150. The operation of patterns was simplified by taking the scheme as a whole for the grant of assistance rather than the different components of individual schemes, as was the practice earlier.

For the Third Plan period, Central assistance in respect to each State was predetermined and communicated to them. The actual entitlement of loans and grants was worked out on the basis of approved Plan schemes and the schematic patterns as done earlier. However, the assistance under loans and grants thus worked out was not necessarily the same as the total assistance indicated for the Annual Plan or the Five Year Plan. In a large number of cases the total assistance indicated was higher than that arrived at on the basis of schematic patterns. In order to give to such States the agreed quantum of assistance, the difference between the total promised assistance and the assistance they were entitled to on the basis of the schematic patterns, was made up through, what was called, 'Miscellaneous Development Loan Assistance'. Certain schemes of a capital nature such as irrigation, power, roads, industries, etc., were approved by the Planning Commission every year for utilization of miscellaneous development loan assistance.

During the discussions on the Draft Fourth Five Year Plan (1966–71) and subsequently, a number of States represented that the patterns of assistance were still cumbersome and involved considerable administrative work and delays. The successive refinements suggested by the Planning Commission did not fully meet the complaints of the States.

Assuming that the rationale of patterns of assistance was to give higher priority to certain schemes and make them more acceptable or tempting to the State Governments for inclusion in their Plans, this purpose would have been served if the total assistance was equal to the sum of assistance earned in accordance with the schematic patterns of assistance. However, the practice was that the total Central assistance was predetermined and if there was a gap between the predetermined amount and the amount earned as a result of patterns of assistance, this came to be filled by miscellaneous development schemes loan. Therefore, the predetermined amount became the vital parameter and the patterns of assistance ceased to have any significance except to the limited extent that the loan-grant mix would get varied. But the loan-grant mix was seldom a serious consideration in the calculations of the States while accepting Central assistance. What was important was the magnitude of assistance. The rationale of different schematic patterns of assistance was, thus, completely defeated by the device of 'miscellaneous development schemes' loan.

However, the fact remained that as a result of the above process a situation arose where financially better off States could so order their affairs that they could get a larger percentage of Central assistance as grant by taking up a larger number of revenue account schemes, which, under the schematic patterns, attracted a larger component of grant assistance. This kind of choice was not available to States whose own resources on revenue account were meagre. This would be evident from the fact that during the Third Five Year Plan, the grant component of Central assistance was 19 per cent in case of Madhya Pradesh and 26 per cent in case of Maharashtra. As a result of this situation, one of the important issues that arose in regard to Central assistance was the loan-grant component of this assistance. It was argued that there should be a uniform and predetermined percentage for these two elements in the total Central assistance.

The position was, therefore, reviewed once again in 1966 and the Planning Commission, after consulting the Central Ministries and State Governments, placed the matter before the National Development Council in August 1966. The NDC appointed a sub-committee to examine the question in greater detail. The patterns approved by the sub-committee were adopted by the Planning Commission and communicated to the States in January 1967. Those patterns were smaller in number and simpler in operation. Central assistance, according to these patterns, generally related to heads, sub-heads, and groups of schemes only, the exception being a few schemes under education and health sectors. The system of ear-marking Central assistance for certain important heads of development or schemes under agriculture and selected projects under irrigation and power, introduced during the Third Plan period, was continued along with these new patterns.

Notwithstanding the simplification and rationalization introduced from the Annual Plan for 1967–8, a few State Governments continued to press the view that there should be greater flexibility in this regard. A modified scheme of channelling aid was suggested to the States in July 1967. This scheme envisaged a provision of earmarked assistance for certain key programmes and projects in the State Plans and a fixed percentage of grants under Social Services and Special Development Programmes for Hill, Border, and Backward Areas. The rest of the programmes in the Plan, it was assumed, could be financed by the States from their own resources. The main objective of this scheme was to reduce the patterns to the minimum in order to give greater flexibility to States in plan formulation and implementation and to encourage them to mobilize additional resources to finance the plans under other sectors.

Most of the States did not consider the new scheme as an improvement over the existing arrangement. In view of the mixed reactions of the States, it was decided that the existing patterns might be continued up to the end of 1968–9 and the whole question be re-examined at the time of formulation of the new Fourth Five Year Plan (1969–74). As was mentioned earlier, there were three Annual Plans for 1966–7, 1967–8 and 1968–9 after the completion of the Third Five Year Plan. The Fourth Plan was to be for the period 1969–74. Its formulation started in 1967 with the new Planning Commission which took over in September 1967.

The State Governments and Central Ministries were asked, in Planning Commission's letter of 8 March 1968, to indicate their views regarding patterns of assistance. Replies received from States and Central Ministries, as also the views expressed by the Administrative Reforms Commission, were taken into consideration by the Committee of Chief Ministers (appointed by the National Development Council in its meeting held in May 1968), which met twice in July and September 1968. This Committee decided to abolish different patterns of assistance attached to specific schemes and to allocate the total Central assistance among block loans and grants. This was expected to give a very large degree of freedom to the States in planning. The National Development Council in its meeting held in April 1969, approved this recommendation of the NDC Committee.

This decision involved complete abolition of scheme-wise patterns as far as State Plan schemes were concerned. It was also decided that each State would receive 30 per cent of the total Central assistance every year as grant and the balance 70 per cent as loan. Central assistance for State Plans was no longer to be related to any individual scheme, group of schemes, or head of development. However, in order to ensure that the priorities of the Plan were generally maintained in the course of implementation, it was decided that *outlays* under certain heads or sub-heads and for a few specific schemes should be *earmarked*.

The procedure for channelling of Central assistance to States for their Annual Plans from 1969–70 onwards was indicated in detail in Planning Commission's letter of 22 May 1969 (Appendix 4.1). The release mechanism adopted for implementing this procedure, is indicated in Appendix 4.2. Some of the highlights of the procedure are:

(i) The Union Ministry of Finance will administer Central assistance for State Plans, excluding the amount to be operated by the National Cooperative Development Corporation. At the time of formulation of the Annual Plans, the Planning Commission indicated the State-wise distribution of Central assistance (on the basis of the objective formula, which came to be known as the Gadgil Formula) for the State's Annual Plan for the concerned year. While intimating the sectoral distribution of the Annual Plan outlay as approved by the Planning Commission, outlays under the Agricultural Programmes and Cooperation, selected irrigation and power schemes, elementary education, rural water supply, etc., are earmarked. The assistance for NCDC schemes was also on the basis of 30 per cent grant and 70 per cent loan. The outlay and assistance for NCDC schemes were intimated separately. The earmarked outlay under NCDC schemes could not be diverted to either Cooperation or any other sector in the Annual Plan outlay. The earmarked outlays under Agriculture and Allied Sectors and Cooperation (excluding NCDC schemes) were taken together and adjustments are permitted within this larger group. If the State Governments envisaged any shortfalls under earmarked sectors, they may propose adjustments so as to reach the Planning Commission before 31 October of the concerned year and obtain the Commission's approval. The State Governments were free to undertake adjustments in outlays in the non-earmarked sectors as they considered necessary, and indicated them to the Planning Commission for formal approval.

(ii) The earmarked outlays and non-earmarked outlays were taken as two separate entities. The total Central assistance was notionally apportioned to these two entities in proportion to their outlays. Excess expenditure on earmarked schemes could make up the shorfall in non-earmarked sectors, but not vice versa.

(iii) A State Government would be able to earn full Central assistance only if the total Plan expenditure equaled or exceeded the approved plan outlay and the expenditure on earmarked schemes/sectors also equaled or exceeded the approved outlay on these schemes/ sectors.

(iv) If the total expenditure falls short of the approved outlay, the State would lose Central assistance proportionately, even if the expenditure on earmarked schemes/sectors equaled or exceeded the approved outlay on them.

(v) Even if the total expenditure equaled or exceeded the total approved outlay on the Annual Plan, the State would lose proportionate Central assistance if the expenditure on earmarked schemes falls short of the approved outlay on them.

(vi) The cut in Central assistance would be under both grants and loans.

Such a procedure was expected to compel the States to ensure that their Plans were purposefully formulated and properly implemented. The condition that there would be reduction in the assistance in proportion to the shortfall in expenditure was expected to act as a deterrent against haphazard or slow implementation of development schemes in priority sectors.

ASSISTANCE FOR HILL AREAS

Special patterns of assistance for Hill Areas in different State Plans were in vogue before the commencement of the Fourth Five Year Plan. There were different patterns of assistance for different areas such as Ladakh, Uttarkhand, Nagaland, Assam Hill Areas, etc. In consultation with the Ministry of Finance, the Planning Commission approved special patterns of assistance for the Fourth Plan of Ladakh, Hill areas of Assam, and Nagaland. Their Central assistance was to comprise 90 per cent grant and 10 per cent loan. The outlays on plans of these hill areas were earmarked under the respective plans of each State each year and could not be diverted. The pattern in the proportionate assistance for the hill areas of Uttar Pradesh, West Bengal and Tamil Nadu was 50 per cent grant and 50 per cent loan. The Annual Plan outlays on these hill areas were to be separately earmarked.

For the Fifth Plan period, the pattern of assistance was 90 per cent grant and 10 per cent loan for the Special Category States of Himachal Pradesh, Manipur, Meghalaya, Nagaland, and Tripura. For the remaining States the pattern was 30 per cent grant and 70 per cent loan. The pattern of assistance for hill areas continued to be the same as in the Fourth Plan period, i.e. 90 per cent grant and 10 per cent loan for Assam hill areas and Ladakh and 50 per cent grant and 50 per cent loan for the hill areas of Uttar Pradesh, West Bengal, and Tamil Nadu.

Thus, the pattern of assistance is 90 per cent grant and 10 per cent loan for all Special Category States.

When the Gadgil Formula first came to be applied in the allocation of Central assistance for the Fourth Five Year Plan period—1969–74, there were 17 States. Out of these, the States of Assam, Jammu & Kashmir, and Nagaland were given special consideration and only the remaining 14 were brought under the ambit of the Gadgil Formula. Later on, when Himachal Pradesh, Manipur, Meghalaya, Sikkim, and Tripura attained statehood, the total number of States went up to 22 for the Fifth Plan period. However, the Gadgil Formula continued to be applied to the earlier 14 States only and all other States were classified as Special Category States and were accorded special treatment as regards allocation and pattern of assistance. As and when new States were formed (they were either Union Territories or carved out of Assam), they were added to the list of Special Category States, with the exception of Goa. There are now 10 Special Category States and 15 Non-special Category States.

UNION TERRITORIES' PLANS

The Union Territories are on an entirely different footing as regards Central assistance. The receipts and expenditure (plan and non-plan) of these Territories form part of the Consolidated Fund of the Government of India. The Territories with legislatures present their own budgets, which are approved by the Ministries of Home Affairs and Finance. The Administrations have considerable revenue account gaps and the Central government meets fully not only the revenue gap on the non-plan side but also the entire plan outlay on both revenue and capital accounts. Hence, the question of scheme-wise patterns of assistance, block loans, and grants, etc., does not arise in the case of Union Territories. The following points clarify the position as it stands now:

(i) The procedure of block loans and block grants is applicable to States only and not to Union Territories.
(ii) Since the entire plan outlays of Union Territories are financed by the Central Government, there is no question of Central assistance for Union Territories, as the term is understood in regard to States.
(iii) Gap in the revenue account (revenue expenditure, both on plan and non-plan accounts *minus* revenue receipts) is met through grants and the gap in capital account (capital expenditure both on plan and non-plan accounts) is met through loans for Union Territories.
(iv) In view of these points, there has never been any question of schematic patterns of assistance for Union Territories.
(v) Schematic patterns of assistance indicated by concerned Central

Ministries as regards Union Territories relate to third party assistance only, i.e. assistance given by the Union Territories to individuals, cooperative societies, etc.

(vi) As in the case of States, there has been earmarking of outlays under certain sectors for Union Territories also during the Fourth Plan period. But its significance is different. In case of States, earmarking of outlays is connected with Central assistance but, in the case of Union Territories, it is only for regulating expenditure priorities.

APPENDIX 4.1

Government of India, Planning Commission
No. PC(P) 4/7/68

New Delhi, the 22nd May 1969,
Jaistha1, 1891 Saka.

To
All State Governments
(Planning and Finance Secretaries)
Sub: Channelling of Central Assistance to the States
for their Annual Plans.

Sir,
The procedure for channelling of Central assistance for schemes included in the State Plans as set out in Planning Commission's Letter No. PC(P)4/2/66, dated January 25, 1967 has been under review for some time. The Committee of the National Development Council recommended at its meeting held in July 1968 that Central assistance to State Governments for their Plan schemes be given in the shape of block loans and grants. After taking into consideration the recommendations made by the Administrative Reforms Commission in this regard as also the views expressed by the State Governments in response to Planning Commission's Letter No. PC(P)4/2/68 dated March 8, 1968, it has been decided, in consultation with the Ministry of Finance, that Central assistance to States for the Fourth Five Year Plan (1969–74), with the exception of funds to be provided by the National Co-operative Development Corporation, will be given as block loans and grants each year. It has been decided that each State should receive 30% of the total assistance every year as a grant, the balance of 70% being loan. The terms and conditions, governing the block loans will be communicated to State Governments separately.

2. Central assistance to the States will not be related to any individual scheme, group of schemes or Head of Development on the basis of matching contribution. However, in order to ensure that the priorities of the Plan are generally maintained in the course of implementation, it has been decided that the outlays under certain Heads or Sub-heads and for a few specified schemes shall be earmarked as indicated below:

(i) Agriculture and allied sectors -*
(excluding Community Development and Panchayats);

*Agricultural production, Minor irrigation, Soil conservation, Area development, Animal husbandry, Dairying and milk supply, Forests, Fisheries, Warehousing and Marketing and Cooperation.

(ii) Specified continuing major irrigation schemes;
(iii) Specified schemes for generation and transmission of power;
(iv) Specified projects not covered under (ii) and (iii) above, involving foreign contractual obligations and inter-State payments;
(v) Elementary Education (classes I to VIII);
(vi) Rural Water Supply programmes.

Outlays for certain specified items of special importance may also be earmarked from time to time in individual States. A list of specified projects under category (ii) to (iv) above, for which outlays will be earmarked, will be communicated separately.

3. The outlays approved for any of the programmes/schemes mentioned in paragraph 2 above would not be divertible to any other programme/scheme. In exceptional cases, for reasons beyond the control of the State Government, if any adjustments become necessary, proposals will be sent to the Planning Commission so as to reach the Commission not later than 31st October of the financial year to which they relate. It will not be possible for the Planning Commission to consider any proposals received after that date.

In respect of other heads of development where the outlays are not earmarked, the State Governments will be free to make inter-se adjustments within a head or sub-head of development. However, the reports of such adjustments should be made to the Commission not later than 15th February of the financial year to which these relate.

4. Central assistance will be payable in full to a State, provided the following two conditions are fulfilled.

(a) The actual expenditure on any individual earmarked item does not fall short of the approved outlay for the same.
(b) The total expenditure on all programmes not covered by (a) above does not fall short of the total approved outlay in respect of the same.

In calculating the Central assistance payable to each State, the expenditure on items under category (a) and (b) above will be reckoned separately in relation to approved outlays. In case there are shortfalls in expenditure under these categories in relation to the approved outlays, Central assistance to which a State Government will be entitled will be, the total of the assistance thus worked out for each of the two categories separately. The reduction will be both under loan and grant, and in the same proportion, which the total Central assistance bears to the total approved Plan outlay.

5. The procedure described above comes into effect from April 1, 1969 and will be valid for the five-year period 1969–70 to 1973–4.

6. The receipt of this letter may kindly be acknowledged.

Yours faithfully,
Sd/-
(B.D. Pande)
Secretary, Planning Commission

Copy forwarded for information to:

1. Ministry of Finance
   (i) Department of Economic Affairs (Budget Division)
   (ii) Department of Expenditure (Plan Finance Division)
2. All other Central Ministries (except Law and Defence)

APPENDIX 4.2

Release Mechanism of Central Assistance for Plans

(a) *Central assistance for State Plan Schemes*:

Ten instalments each representing 1/12th of the amount allocated for State Plan are released every month from April to January and the balance is released towards the end of February–March on the basis of progress of expenditure.

(b) *Additional Central assistance for Externally Aided Projects*:

Releases are made in four instalments for each quarter ending June, September, December and March.

(c) *Central assistance for Centrally Sponsored Schemes*:

Until the end of 1976–77, the procedure was that eight instalments of Ways and Means Advances, each representing 1/12th of the amount of assistance allocated for Centrally sponsored Schemes were released by the Ministry of Finance (Plan Finance Division) every month from April to November towards expenditure on Centrally Sponsored Schemes. Thereafter, regular sanctions were issued by the Administrative Ministries on the basis of the progress of expenditure reported by the State Governments, after adjustments of Ways and Means Advances already sanctioned.

The above procedure was discontinued with effect from 1st April 1977 and since then the Central Ministries themselves have been releasing funds directly to the State Governments for Centrally Sponsored Schemes. At that time, there was no firm schedule of releases to the State Governments by the Central Ministries. They were, however, advised to ensure regular flow of funds to the States by releasing funds each month or quarter on *ad hoc* basis and thereafter follow up the requirements of obtaining progress of expenditure, etc., so as to enable themselves to make the final releases at the end of the financial year.

5

Centrally Sponsored Schemes

The word 'Centrally Sponsored Schemes' is self explanatory in the sense that these schemes are sponsored by the Central Government (in various Ministries), and not initiated by the States as such. Central assistance made available to the States for these schemes is different from and over and above the Central assistance for State plan schemes.

As has been stated in Chapter 3, the decisions taken by the National Development Council in its meeting held in May 1969, based on the recommendations of the NDC Committee, covered the issue of quantum of outlays on Centrally Sponsored Schemes also. We propose to deal with this topic in detail in this chapter.

No clear cut principles were evolved in the beginning, either for defining the Centrally Sponsored Schemes (CSS) or for determining their outlays under different development sectors in the First Five Year Plan. Initially, a number of development schemes were being executed by the States outside their Plans during the First Plan period, but there was no mention of the category of CSS in the First Five Year Plan Document. At the end of the First Plan when a large number of such schemes (outside the Plan) were transferred to the State Sector, a new classification of CSS was introduced to cover the remaining schemes. This classification appeared for the first time in the *Second Five-Year Plan Document*:

> The classification of outlay between the Centre and the States in the Second Five-Year Plan is a little different from that followed in the First Five Year Plan. In the First Plan, in addition to the schemes to be implemented by the Central ministries, a number of programmes, which were sponsored and assisted by the Central Government through various Ministries, were shown in the Central Sector. Expenditure found on a matching basis by the States for these schemes was, however, intended to form part of the State plans. This led to certain difficulties in the presentation of Plans. In the Second Five Year Plan, the general principle followed is that Plans of States

should include, to the maximum extent possible, all programmes to be implemented by them or public authorities or local boards set up by them. The fact that for any particular programme carried out in the States, either the whole or part of the resources comes from the Central Government or agencies set up by it does not, as a rule, affect the principle that programmes should be included in the State Plan. While this principle has been generally applied, at this stage there are a few items, which belong to State Plans, but some part of the expenditure is still shown at the Centre, for instance, in housing, welfare of backward classes, and village and small industries. Part of the amounts shown at the Centre is likely to be allocated between the States when certain proposals or other details, which are under consideration, have been agreed upon. (*Second Five-Year Plan Document*, Chapter III)

Principles for selection of certain schemes as Centrally Sponsored Schemes were not spelt out, but one parameter was evident from the above, i.e. schemes, whose State-wise allocation was not definitive at the time of finalization of the Plan, could find a place in the category of Centrally Sponsored Schemes.

The desire of the Planning Commission to restrict the categories of schemes that could be sponsored by the Central Ministries was evident from the following:

Provisions in the States and at the Centre have been made on the principle that generally development schemes to be implemented by State Governments should form part of the State Plans and only certain limited categories of schemes should be shown in the plans of Central Ministries as being 'sponsored' by the Central Government. (*Third Five-Year Plan*, Chapter V)

At the end of the Third Five Year Plan, there were as many as 92 Centrally Sponsored Schemes with varying patterns of assistance. For most of the schemes, the prescribed patterns were rather complicated, in that, for a number of such schemes, the staffing patterns, scales of pay, designs of buildings, details of equipment, etc., were laid down which were often at variance with those prevalent in the States.

Preparations for the formulation of the Fourth Five Year Plan, 1966–71 started in the second half of 1963. According to the tentative schedule of work, the Draft Outline of the Fourth Plan was to be ready by early 1965 and the final Draft before April 1966.

The National Development Council met in August 1966 to consider the 'Draft Outline of the Fourth Five-Year Plan 1966–71'. It was stated in Chapter 1 of the Draft Outline that a final view had yet to be taken on the classification of Plan schemes as between Centrally sponsored, Centrally aided, and State Plan schemes. The broad approach of the Planning Commission, however, was (vide agenda papers for the NDC meeting held on 20 and 21 August 1966) that principal criteria for classification of plan schemes as Centrally sponsored might be:

(i) A limited number of important schemes to be implemented as matters of national policy such as Family Planning, Resettlement of landless agricultural workers, etc.
(ii) Schemes such as those for specialized research and training, which would benefit more than one State or might be of all-India importance.
(iii) Pilot projects for research and development; and
(iv) New schemes introduced after the Plan had been finalized.

The National Development Council, in its meeting held in August 1966, appointed a sub-committee which went into the issue in detail. The sub-committee agreed with the suggestions of the Planning Commission and decided that some of the schemes classified as Centrally Sponsored Schemes in the Draft Outline should be classified as 'Centrally Aided Schemes' and that the number of Centrally Sponsored Schemes should be reduced to the minimum.

In the light of the decisions of the NDC, the Planning Commission held discussions with the Central Ministries and finalized the list of Centrally Sponsored Schemes, which was communicated to the States in January 1967. Even after transfer of 36 schemes, originally classified as Centrally Sponsored Schemes in the Draft Outline, to the State Plan sector, the number of Centrally Sponsored Schemes still stood at 90 in 1967. Of these, 60 were eligible for 100 per cent assistance, 12 schemes for 75 per cent, 3 schemes for 60 per cent, and 15 schemes for 50 per cent assistance.

The effect of a series of external factors delayed the whole process of formulation of the Fourth Five Year Plan. The Planning Commission was reconstituted in September 1967 and it was felt that many of the assumptions and estimates of the Draft Outline (for 1966–71) were no longer valid and fresh exercises would have to be undertaken. The Commission also felt that the Fourth Five Year Plan should commence from 1969–70 and the Plans for 1966–7, 1967–8, and 1968–9 should be treated as Annual Plans. The National Development Council in its meeting held in December 1967, accepted these views.

In their letter of 8 March 1968, the Planning Commission asked the States to indicate their views regarding

(a) patterns of Central assistance to States; and
(b) classification of plan schemes for the new Fourth Five-Year Plan for 1969–74.

Views of the States and the Central Ministries, as summarized in Agenda Paper III of the NDC meeting held in May 1968, were as follows:

VIEWS OF STATES

Many States suggested that the number of Centrally Sponsored Schemes should be considerably reduced and those that might continue should be given 100 % assistance. There should be flexibility in regard to pay scales, staffing patterns, designs of buildings, etc. The Government of Kerala suggested complete abolition of this category of schemes. Uttar Pradesh suggested fixation of the five year outlay for these schemes for individual States, annual plan allocations being indicated at the time of the Annual Plan discussions.

VIEWS OF CENTRAL MINISTRIES

All the Ministries have suggested the continuation of the existing Centrally Sponsored Schemes. The Department of Labour and Employment has, however, recommended that the CSS of that Department should be transferred to the State sector.

Ministries of Food and Agriculture, Health, and Works, Housing & Urban Development have suggested an addition of 15 new schemes to the existing list. Six schemes, which were earlier agreed to be transferred to State Plans, have now been proposed to be classified as Centrally sponsored.

Ministry of Health has proposed that 8 schemes relating to the Control of Communicable Diseases and Primary Health Centres, which were earlier classified as Centrally aided, be now transferred to the Centrally sponsored sector.

The Ministry of Education have suggested recasting of the Centrally Sponsored Schemes in their sector.

The views of the Ministry of Home Affairs are almost the same as those of the State Governments as regards classification of Centrally Sponsored Schemes, the manner of financing them, flexibility to be given to the States in regard to staffing patterns, pay scales, designs of buildings, etc., in respect of these schemes.

RECOMMENDATIONS OF ARC

The Administrative Reforms Commission has made the following recommendations regarding Centrally Sponsored Schemes:

1. The number of Centrally Sponsored Schemes should be kept to the minimum;
2. The selection of the schemes should be made strictly on the basis of the following criteria:
   - (a) they should relate to demonstrations, pilot projects, surveys and research;
   - (b) they should have a regional or inter-State character;
   - (c) they should require lump sum provisions to be made until they could be broken down territorially; and
   - (d) they should have an overall significance from the all-India angle.

In the agenda papers just referred to, the National Development Council was requested to express its views on the following issues as regards the Centrally Sponsored Schemes:

- (i) Should there be Centrally Sponsored Schemes at all? If so, what should be the criteria for selection of schemes for inclusion in this category?
- (ii) Should all the Centrally Sponsored Schemes carry 100 per cent assistance? Or should the State Governments be asked to provide a matching share in respect of some schemes?
- (iii) Should the outlays on the Centrally Sponsored Schemes be predetermined for individual States for the Plan period as a whole?

(iv) It was often felt that conditions attached to the Centrally Sponsored Schemes were too rigid. What kind of conditions should be attached to such schemes as regards to (a) Staffing patterns, (b) scales of pay, (c) standard designs for buildings, (d) provision of equipment, and (e) supervision and inspection?

The National Development Council, in its meeting held in May 1968, reviewed the position. The Committee appointed by the NDC in this meeting, considered the various issues in depth and recommended a list of 52 schemes to be retained as compared to the original 92 Centrally Sponsored Schemes. Subsequently, the Planning Commission and the Ministry of Food, Agriculture, Community Development and Cooperation, decided that the 7 schemes to be administered by the ICAR may be classified as purely Central Schemes, with the result that in the Fourth Five Year Plan (1969–74) the total number of Centrally Sponsored Schemes was 45. The Centrally Sponsored Schemes were mainly under agriculture, health, family planning, and welfare of backward classes. The Committee of the NDC also recommended that the Centrally Sponsored Schemes would be limited in total value to 1/6 of the quantum of Central Plan assistance to States, and the Centre would wholly finance all the schemes. It was also decided that the Centrally Sponsored Schemes should fulfil the following criteria:

(a) that they relate to demonstrations, pilot projects, surveys, and research;
(b) that they have a regional or inter-State character;
(c) that they require lump sum provisions to be made until they could be broken down territorially; and
(d) that they have an over all significance from the all-India angle.

In spite of these decisions of the National Development Council, the Administrative Ministries at the Centre continued introducing new schemes as Centrally Sponsored Schemes in the Fourth Plan itself. This was more so during the Fifth Five Year Plan. The Ministries introduced new schemes sometimes without much justification and in violation of the approved criteria. The States also, during this period, did not object since the schemes were financed 100 per cent by the Centre.

After the 1977 general elections, the Janata Government replaced the Congress Government and terminated the Fifth Plan (1974–9) by 1977–8, i.e. in four years only. Preparations were on for the formulation of a 'Rolling Plan'. When the NDC, in its meeting held in March 1978, appointed a Committee to go into the matter of Centre-State relations with special reference to a review of the Gadgil Formula and a re-examination of the Centrally Sponsored Schemes, this issue came up again for examination.

The Chief Ministers argued that though most of the Centrally Sponsored Schemes were useful, they should be in the State Plan and that an enlargement of these schemes reduced the amount of Central assistance available for State Plans. The Central Ministries, on the other hand, insisted that there were many innovative schemes like the Command Area Development Agency (CADA), Small Farmers Development Agency (SFDA), Drought Prone Areas Programme (DPAP), Marginal Farmers and Agricultural Labour (WAL), etc., where, but for the Centre's initiative, the development efforts of the States would have been inadequate and that the Centrally Sponsored Schemes were also meant to achieve a degree of uniformity in priority areas in different States.

According to the information furnished by the Planning Commission to the Committee of the NDC, there were 116 Centrally Sponsored Schemes under implementation in the year 1978–9. In addition, a further 74 schemes came up in another category and were said to be Central Schemes, which were in the nature of Centrally Sponsored Schemes. These later came to be called Central Sector Schemes. This was a device to try to show that the limit of 1/6 in the Gadgil Formula was not exceeded. It was argued that Centrally Sponsored Schemes figured in the State budget with matching Central assistance on the receipts side. A Central Sector Scheme, on the other and, was entirely in the Central budget, though it was intended to be implemented by the States. The argument was that if the Centre chose to provide for such schemes within its own budget, no limits could be prescribed, other than the limit of budgetary resource. The outlay on these two categories of schemes far exceeded the limit of 1/6 of the total quantum of Central assistance for State Plans, which was agreed to in 1968 as part of the Gadgil Formula.

The first meeting of the NDC Committee (referred to earlier) was held in August 1978. The Committee appointed a Working Group to discuss in detail, its terms of reference. The Working Group met thrice. The second meeting of the NDC Committee was held in January 1979 to consider the recommendations of the Working Group. The following was a report by Dr. D.T. Lakdawala, Deputy Chairman, Planning Commission, on the deliberations of the NDC Committee:

On the question of Centrally Sponsored Schemes, it was agreed at the Working Group stage, that a detailed review should be made of the Centrally Sponsored Schemes with a view to ensuring a substantial reduction in their number and bring down the outlay on them from an estimated level of Rs. 6,000 crores to at least Rs. 3,500 crores without affecting the major objectives of the Plan. A 'Committee of Officials' under the chairmanship of Secretary, Planning Commission was appointed for the purpose. His report, summarising the broad consensus or the majority opinion, as it emerged at the meetings was, that:

(i) Centrally Sponsored Schemes of the magnitude of Rs. 600 crores need not be continued, as the States would be expected to take care of them. It was, of course, not implied in this recommendation that these schemes did not serve any purpose, but only that the objectives could be equally fulfilled by the States being left free to decide on their own without any direct guidance from or participation by the Centre;

(ii) It was possible to effect a saving of the order of Rs. 400 crores by reducing the estimated outlay on certain schemes;

(iii) Schemes like Family Planning, Prevention of Malaria, Control of Communicable Diseases, Construction of inter-State Transmission Lines, etc., should continue to be Centrally Sponsored Schemes on a 100% assistance basis. The estimated expenditure on these would be around Rs. 1,700 crores;

(iv) Schemes for weaker sections, agricultural labour and rural development (SFDA, WAL, CADA, RMNP, etc.), estimated to cost Rs. 3,300 crores, should remain as Centrally Sponsored Schemes but financed on a sharing basis. This modification would mean a saving of Rs. 1,650 crores in Central outlay.

The recommendations would imply retention of Rs. 3,350 crores worth of Centrally Sponsored Schemes out of a total of Rs. 6,000 crores that were originally estimated to be incurred on them. (Schemes worth Rs. 600 crores transferred to State Plan sector, Rs. 400 crores saving on account of reduction in outlay on certain schemes and saving of Rs. 1,650 crores by changing the pattern of certain schemes to a matching basis.) Of the saving of Rs. 2,650 crores released thereby, Rs. 2,000 crores would be available as additional block assistance for State Plans for the period 1979–83.

The Working Group also recommended an important change in the procedure for operation of the Centrally Sponsored Schemes. The Central Government should lay down only broad guidelines, leaving the detailed sanctions to the States. The States' Annual Plan discussions should cover all such schemes and provision for them should be made from the beginning instead of piecemeal approvals throughout the year. This would make it possible for the States to treat the Centrally Sponsored Schemes as part of the State Plan as per the suggestion made by the Working Group.

The States generally welcomed the idea of reducing the scope of the Centrally Sponsored Schemes, though some of them had differences of opinion on which particular schemes should be retained. Some of them did not like the idea of the Centrally Sponsored Schemes being financed on a matching basis. Area development schemes like SFDA, MFAL, CADA, and DPAP were now merged with the IRDP, and those pertaining to RMNP were to play a very vital part in the strategy of the Draft Sixth Plan in its fight against unemployment and poverty. It was felt that these programmes should be properly financed and there should be uniformity in the broad approach to counter these problems. On the question of whether financing of some schemes on a matching basis served any purpose, the Planning Commission felt that, firstly it guarded, to some extent, against overstaffing and inefficient expenditure and secondly, the States would have the freedom to choose from a bunch of Centrally Sponsored Schemes administered on a matching basis.

On the recommendations of the NDC Committee and the decisions of the National Development Council, the Centrally Sponsored Schemes included in the Draft Sixth Plan (1978–83) and

Central Sector Schemes in the nature of Centrally Sponsored Schemes, were divided into three categories:

(a) Schemes, which would continue to be Centrally sponsored, with 100 per cent assistance;
(b) Schemes which would continue to be Centrally sponsored, with expenditure to be shared between the Centre and the States; and
(c) 70 schemes, which would cease to be Centrally sponsored.

As indicated earlier, the Fifth Five Year Plan (1974–9) was terminated one year earlier by the Janata Government, which came into power at the Centre in 1977. The Sixth Plan (1978–83) on the 'Rolling Plan' concept, was formulated by the Janata Government, which stayed in power for hardly two years. A new government came into power at the Centre in 1979. Plans for 1978–9 and 1979–80 were treated as Annual Plans and a new Sixth Five Year Plan was formulated for the period 1980–5.

In spite of the decisions of the National Development Council, in its meeting held in February 1979, to reduce the number and quantum of allocation for Centrally Sponsored Schemes, the Sixth Plan witnessed a further enlargement of such schemes both in terms of number and the quantum of assistance. Many Chief Ministers were complaining in the NDC meetings and also outside, against the large increase in the flow of assistance for Centrally Sponsored Schemes. The National Development Council, while considering the Document on Approach to the Seventh Five Year Plan, at its meeting in July 1984, decided that a Committee of Experts may be set up to go into some specific issues and make recommendations there on. One of the issues so identified by the NDC was: 'The scope and role of Centrally Sponsored Schemes in sectoral development plans.'

Accordingly, an Expert Committee under the Chairmanship of Sri K. Ramamurthi, former Chief Secretary of Orissa, was set up in August 1984, to go into the issue and make suitable recommendations.

EXPERT COMMITTEE 1984

The terms of reference of the Expert Committee were:

1. The National Development Council, in its meeting held in 1968, decided that Centrally Sponsored Schemes should be limited to 1/6 of the quantum of Central Plan assistance to the States. This was reiterated by the NDC in 1979. In the context of the Approach to the Seventh Five-Year Plan 1985–90, is there any need to review this ceiling and if so, on what basis this review is made?
2. Do the criteria laid down in 1968 by the NDC for Centrally Sponsored Schemes require a review?

The criteria laid down were:

(a) that they relate to demonstrations, pilot projects, surveys and research;
(b) that they have a regional or inter-State character;
(c) that they require lump sum provision to be made until they could be broken down territorially; and
(d) that they have an overall significance from the all-India angle.

3. Whether, keeping in mind the background to the decision of the NDC in 1979 to reduce the number and coverage of Centrally Sponsored Schemes, there is need to review the number and coverage of Centrally Sponsored Schemes in the context of the Seventh Five-Year Plan 1985–90, and the funding and administrative pattern that should govern such schemes?

The Expert Committee submitted its report in January 1985.

As there was no centralized agency in the Government of India, which had complete information regarding the Centrally Sponsored Schemes under implementation, the Committee had to obtain this from various administrative Ministries. The Committee prepared an elaborate questionnaire for eliciting details (numbers, outlays, etc.) on Centrally Sponsored Schemes and views of the Ministries and States on the terms of reference. The views of the Ministries and States are given in Appendix 5.1.

In 1969, their number was 45. At the time of finalization of the Sixth Plan (1978–83) it had increased to 190, which was decided to be reduced to 75 by the NDC in 1979.

Assistance for the Centrally Sponsored Schemes, which was Rs.1,238 crores in 1980–1, increased to Rs. 3,004 crores in 1984–5. During the Sixth Plan period 1980–5, a total assistance of Rs. 9,318 crores was allocated to CSS, which worked out to 35 per cent of the total assistance to the States. This was far in excess of the 1/6 stipulated by the National Development Council in 1968 at the time of finalization of the Gadgil Formula.

The report of the Expert Committee made many interesting and important observations, a few of which can be highlighted here.

(i) There was no centralized agency in the Government of India, which had complete information regarding the Centrally Sponsored Schemes under implementation.

(ii) Though decisions were taken from time to time to reduce the number of CSS, the schemes, in actual practice, had been increasing over the years. In 1969 their number was 45. At the time of finalization of the Sixth Plan (1978–83) it was 190, which was decided to be reduced to 75 by the NDC in 1979.

(iii) Assistance for Centrally Sponsored Schemes, which was Rs. 1,238 crores in 1980–1, increased to Rs. 3,004 crores in 1984–5.

(iv) The outlay of Rs. 3,916 crores for CSS indicated for the Sixth Plan 1978–83 was increased to Rs. 9,318 crores for the Sixth Plan 1980–5 (replacing the earlier Plan). This was 35 per cent of total Central assistance for State plans, far in excess of 1/6 stipulated by the NDC in 1968 at the time of the finalization of the Gadgil Formula, even though there was no overt policy decision to alter the earlier decision of the NDC to reduce the quantum of assistance flowing through the CSS.

(v) As against 75 CSS at the beginning of the Sixth Plan (1980–5), there were 201 schemes at the end of the Sixth Plan. Table 5.1 gives details, Ministry-wise.

(vi) Out of the 201 schemes in the Sixth Plan, 13 had an outlay of over Rs. 100 crores each, together accounting for nearly 80 per cent of the total flow of assistance. There were 57 schemes with an outlay of Rs. 1 crore each and 55 with an outlay between Rs. 1 crore and Rs. 5 crores. Agriculture had the largest number

TABLE 5.1: CENTRALLY SPONSORED SCHEMES—SIXTH PLAN 1980–5

Ministry	*No. of schemes*	*Allocation during 1980–5 (Rs. crores)*
Agriculture	53	879
Health	21	1,924
Home Affairs	12	852
Industry	11	889
Rural development	12	2,772
Works and Housing	7	910
Irrigation	7	378
Others	78	715
Total	201	9,319

of schemes but its share in the assistance for the CSS was 9.5 per cent only.

(vii) Only a few schemes account for the bulk of the transfers and any attempt to substantially reduce the assistance for CSS would have to affect these schemes.

(viii) On the basis of the information available, it was found that relatively backward States like Bihar, Uttar Pradesh, Orissa, and Rajasthan were receiving per capita assistance (for the CSS) less than what they would have got under the Gadgil Formula, had these amounts been transferred to the assistance for the State Plan. Relatively developed States benefited more through the CSS.

(ix) Since a major portion of the assistance was for schemes with matching patterns, States with better financial resources were able to get a larger share of the CSS.

(x) The Committee did not agree with the views of the Central Ministries that:

(a) the national goals and objectives can be achieved only through the CSS;

(b) the States do not implement such programmes unless there is a financial incentive; and

(c) the States do not part with information regarding implementation of plan programmes.

(xi) The Committee was of the view that the Central Ministries evince interest only in schemes, which are implemented as Centrally Sponsored Schemes, and their appreciation of the State Plan is often fragmentary.

(xii) The schemes that were transferred to State Plans in 1979 immediately lost their 'national importance' as far as the Central Ministries were concerned, since they were no longer the CSS.

The Expert Committee recommended as follows:

1. Centrally Sponsored Schemes had an important role to play, but their number should be limited and they should primarily aim at a process of change.
2. The schemes should satisfy one of the following criteria:

(a) they should relate to demonstration, pilot projects, survey, and research;
(b) should have a regional or inter-State character;
(c) should aim at building up institutional framework for the country as a whole or for a region; or
(d) should be in the nature of a pacesetter with a definite time frame within which the objectives are sought to be realized.

3. Programmes of national importance could be identified and classified into a sub-plan within the State Plan with earmarked outlays and special Central assistance.
4. Outlay for the CSS should not exceed 1/6 of the total Central assistance to States. However, if the Committee's recommendation in point 3 was not accepted, it in any case should not exceed 1/3.
5. Any schemes having less than Rs. 25 crores with an all-India coverage or less than Rs. 10 crores with a coverage of a few States only, should not be taken up as a Centrally Sponsored Scheme.
6. Schemes, whose committed liability at the end of their operation would fall on the States, should invariably be classified as CSS. Schemes, which are essentially Centrally sponsored, should not be classified as Central Sector Schemes.
7. All CSS should be identified at the time of plan formulation together with likely outlays and pattern of financing.

8. CSS introduced in the middle of a Plan period should be fully financed by the Centre.
9. CSS should be reviewed at the time of annual plan discussions.
10. Prior clearance of the State Finance and Planning Departments for introducing new CSS should be insisted on by the Central Ministries.
11. There should be close coordination between the Central Ministries and State Governments regarding the objectives and administrative procedures for implementing the CSS.
12. Financial sanctions for the CSS should be issued by the Expenditure Finance Committee, so that there is a Central Agency, which possesses all the information on the CSS.
13. There should be an effective mechanism for coordination between various Central institutions like the UGC, ICAR, CSIR, etc., and the States to ensure that there are adequate outlays in the State Plan to receive and assimilate development schemes administered through such agencies.
14. An effective information system may be developed for transmission of information regarding innovative schemes like the Employment Guarantee Scheme, Midday Meals Scheme, etc., taken up by different States so that other States can also adopt them if found suitable.

It will be seen that shorn of the rhetoric, the Expert Committee, in effect, recommended an increase of the original limit for the Centrally Sponsored Schemes from 1/6 of the State plan assistance to 1/3.

The report of the Expert Committee was considered in the meeting of the National Development Council held in November 1985. The following is a relevant extract from the summary record of this meeting.

> As regards Ramamurti Committee report on the future of Centrally Sponsored Schemes, several divergent views have been expressed. He (Deputy Chairman, Planning Commission) felt that there was a strong feeling among States that the number of Centrally Sponsored Schemes ought to be reduced. To decide the various issues like the number of Centrally Sponsored Schemes to be retained or dropped, what to do with the resultant

savings and the manner of their distribution among the States, etc., he (Deputy Chairman) requested the Council to accept the Planning Commission's recommendation that a Committee of the NDC might be set up to go into all the issues and report back to it with its recommendations. Depending on the agreement reached on the future of Centrally Sponsored Schemes, the Seventh Plan could, if the Council so desired, be modified. To ensure that the Committee was a balanced one, the Prime Minister, as Chairman of the Council, was authorised by the NDC to finalise the composition of the Committee. (Summary Record of NDC meeting, November 1985, p. 43)

Accordingly, a Committee under the Chairmanship of Sri P.V. Narasimha Rao, the then Union Minister of Human Resources Development, was set up. The Committee included three Union Ministers, 11 Chief Ministers, and Sri Raja J. Chellaiah, Member, Planning Commission, as the Member Secretary. The terms of reference of the Committee were:

(i) Review the criteria laid down by the National Development Council in 1979, for taking up of the Centrally Sponsored Schemes, and suggest modifications therein, or additional criteria, that should govern such schemes for the future.
(ii) Review the question whether the total outlays (Central outlays plus States' outlays on the CSS) should be limited to 1/6 or 1/7 of the total Central plan assistance to the States in any given plan period, or there is need to modify this ceiling keeping in view the Plan objectives (among others) of poverty alleviation and employment generation.
(iii) Suggest the consultation modalities between the Centre and the States that should be operative when the question of sanctioning new Centrally Sponsored Schemes is mooted by any Union Ministry or State Government.
(iv) List all the Centrally Sponsored Schemes that were under implementation on 1 April 1985 and consider which schemes were needed to be continued, dropped, or transferred to the State Governments for implementation; and for those schemes to be transferred, the modalities of transfer, including the formula that would govern the transfer to individual States of the funds involved.

(v) Suggest a periodical review mechanism of transferred schemes, so that achievement of national plan objectives involved in the scheme is watched jointly by the Centre and the States.

It is evident from the terms of reference that they were biased in favour of continuing the existing policy concerning the Centrally Sponsored Schemes as regards magnitude and criteria, in spite of the near-unanimous objections of States on these two points.

The first meeting of this Committee of the NDC on Centrally Sponsored Schemes was held in November 1986. The Committee was of the view that the criteria suggested by the Ramamurti Committee seemed to be too broad and did not cover the fulfilment of an important national objective like poverty alleviation. The Committee adopted the following criteria for the Centrally Sponsored Schemes.

1. The fulfilment of an important national objective such as poverty alleviation or achievement of minimum standards in education; or
2. The programme had a regional or inter-State character; or
3. The programme or scheme should be in the nature of a pacesetter or should relate to demonstration, survey, or research.

The Committee recommended that schemes other than these might be considered for transfer to the States.

These decisions of the Committee, taken in its first meeting itself, reflected the bias of the Government of India on this entire question. Therefore, it could not be assumed that the Committee would deal with the issues raised by the States in an objective manner. It was taken for granted that the Centre could formulate any scheme relating to any subject as Centrally sponsored irrespective of whether the subject was allotted to the States under the Constitution. The basic approach that all subjects allotted to the States would be in the State Plan and that the role of the Centre in such subjects should be a restricted one based on a selective approach was abandoned. It was assumed that 'any important national objective' could be dealt with sincerely and effectively only by the Centre. The allocation of subjects in the Constitution between the States and the Centre could be passed over by merely describing any subject as of 'national importance'. It was almost as if Entry 97, in List I of the Seventh Schedule was amended to read as: '97. Any other matter not enumerated in List II or List III, or any other so enumerated, but deemed by the Union to be of national importance. . . .'

The criteria adopted were so general and all encompassing that the Committee's recommendation for transferring a few unimportant schemes to the State Plan sector, made its entire exercise a mere charade.

The Committee, in its first meeting, further decided to constitute a Group of Officials to work out the details, as per the decisions arrived at by the Committee. The Group of Officials was constituted in April 1986 under the Chairmanship of Secretary to the Planning Commission. The terms of reference of the Group were:

(i) to list all the Centrally Sponsored Schemes that were under implementation on 1 April 1985 and to consider which of these schemes need to be continued, dropped, or transferred, the modalities of transfer including the formula for transfer of concerned amounts to the States;
(ii) to suggest the modalities for taking up new Centrally Sponsored Schemes;
(iii) to suggest a periodical review of transferred schemes, so that achievement of national plan objectives involved in the schemes is watched jointly by the Centre and the States.

The Group of Officials met four times and submitted its report in April 1987. A summary of recommendations of the Group is given in Appendix 5.1.

According to the analysis of the Group, out of the total 262 Centrally Sponsored Schemes in existence as on 1 April 1985, 140 were continuing from the Sixth Plan and 122 were introduced during the Seventh Plan. As against the total outlay of Rs. 15,757 crores on these 262 schemes, the Group recommended retention of 149 schemes with a Seventh Plan outlay of Rs. 14,496 crores and the transfer of the remaining amount to the States from 1 April 1988 (i.e. for the remaining two years of the Seventh Plan), to be distributed on the basis of the Modified Gadgil Formula. The Group felt that it might not be practical to lay down any ceiling on the

Centrally Sponsored Schemes. The Group merely hoped that a rigorous procedure, for ensuring that the criteria for schemes proposed by the NDC Committee were fulfilled, would be sufficient to keep the propensity for proliferation of such schemes in check.

The Group recommended that 113 schemes with a Seventh Plan outlay of Rs. 1,261 crores and a balance outlay of Rs. 800 crores during 1988–90, may be transferred to the States. (This was, however, not done.) Since the scheme by scheme examination based on the NDC Committee's criteria disclosed that schemes with an outlay of about 92 per cent of the total outlay of Rs. 15,757 crores would require to be retained, the Group did not consider it practical to recommend any ceiling by way of a fixed percentage of Central assistance to State Plans, as compared to the 1/6 recommended under the original Gadgil Formula or 1/3 suggested by the Ramamurti Committee.

Table 5.2 brings out certain highlights of the Group's recommendations.

Under the criteria of poverty alleviation and human resources development, the Group managed to retain schemes with an overwhelming outlay (92 per cent) under the Centrally Sponsored sector.

The report of the Group of Officials set up by the NDC

TABLE 5.2: RECOMMENDATIONS OF THE GROUP OF OFFICIALS

(Outlays in Rs. crores)

Sector	*Recommended to be*				*Total*	
	Retained		*Transferred*		*No.*	*Outlay*
	No.	*Outlay*	*No.*	*Outlay*		
1. Agri. and Co-op.	64	1,049	35	667	99	1,716
2. Health and Family Welfare	9	3,790	6	23	15	3,813
3. Rural Development	13	5,946	6	90	19	6,036
4. Social Welfare	12	779	6	41	18	820
5. Education	13	462	–	–	13	462
6. Other sectors	38	2,470	60	440	98	2,970
Total	149	14,496	113	1,261	262	15,757

Source: Report of the Group of Officials appointed by the Committee of the National Development Council.

Committee was submitted in April 1987. The NDC Committee on Centrally Sponsored Schemes met on 4 August 1987. Chief Ministers of various States again reiterated their position regarding the ever increasing number and scope of the Centrally Sponsored Schemes in sectors which are primarily the constitutional responsibility of the States. States were very critical of the various recommendations of the Group regarding the number of schemes and outlays to be retained, transfers to be effective from the Eighth Plan, non-feasibility of placing any ceiling on the numbers and financial outlays of Centrally Sponsored Schemes, etc.

No decision was taken as regards transfer of any Centrally Sponsored Schemes during the Seventh Plan period.

Consequent on the change of governments at the Centre and in many States in November 1989 elections, preparations for a new Eighth Five Year Plan were started by a newly constituted Planning Commission. The Planning Commission prepared a note on 'Distribution of Central Budget Support for States' Plan Expenditure' (refer to Appendix 4.1), in July 1990 in which they had the following to say on Centrally Sponsored Schemes:

> Over the years, the role of CSS has increased very sharply. In the context of restoring federal principle and for paving the way for decentralisation below the State level to facilitate comprehensive area planning and implementation, the Eighth Plan Approach paper has spelt out the need for a drastic revision in the CSS regime. Consistent with that policy, an attempt has to be made to free the major part of those funds from strict regulation by the different Central Ministries. Instead, the maximum possible decentralisation, keeping clearly the national objectives in view, has to be attempted. At the same time, reasonable checks have to be put in place to remove any apprehension that funds may be diverted from programmes of national importance.
>
> Schemes, which it is finally decided are to be retained as Centrally Sponsored Schemes, will continue under the same arrangement as of now. Funds for the other schemes, which are to be transferred to the States, may be added to the block assistance as 85% grant and 15% loan (as most of the assistance for Centrally Sponsored Schemes now is given as grants). However, the utilisation of funds for schemes of national priority will need to be earmarked. It is further suggested that 5% of these funds may be retained, by the Central Ministry concerned, for giving technical and research support and for evaluation. The Finance Ministry as in the case of State Plan block

assistance will make release of funds for these schemes. Wherever the funds are to be spent by local bodies, this would also be indicated, along with the criteria, at the time of the transfer of funds from the Centre to the States.

This was considered by the forty-second meeting of the NDC held in October 1990. The following is an extract from the summary record of this meeting:

The Prime Minister stated that they were actively considering further decentralisation of the Centrally Sponsored Schemes. The Planning Commission had very strongly recommended it. The Government was also actively considering it. He added: 'We want to make it clear that there should not be decentralisation only from the Centre to the State capital. That is not the central idea. Therefore, the commitment from the Chief Ministers has to come that this will be further decentralised to the Panchayat level or the appropriate level with a particular scheme of improvement. With this genuine decentralisation, people would get the benefit.

There was a change of Government at the Centre again in December 1990 and the Planning Commission was also re-constituted.

At the National Development Council meeting held in January 1997, to discuss the Draft Approach to the Ninth Five Year Plan, several Chief Ministers were of the opinion that the Centrally Sponsored Schemes should be transferred to the States along with the resources, especially those falling within the purview of the State List as per the Constitution and retention of the CSS be limited to those as identified by the Approach Paper to the Ninth Five Year Plan. On this issue, the Approach Paper stated that: 'In principle, Centrally Sponsored Schemes should be confined to schemes of an inter-State character; matters impinging on national security; selected national priorities where Central supervision is essential for effective implementation; and externally financed multi-State projects where Central co-ordination is necessary for operational reasons.'

The Ninth Five Year Plan Document also reiterated the same. The following is an extract from Volume I of *Ninth Five Year Plan* for 1997–2002.

TRANSFER OF CENTRALLY SPONSORED SCHEMES

6.10. Another issue, which has been cropping up from time to time in the relations between the Centre and the States, pertains to the Centrally Sponsored Schemes (CSS). The CSS are being implemented right from the beginning of the First Plan. When they were conceived, they were welcomed as they were intended to serve certain specific national goals. One classic example of CSS, which has made a far-reaching impact, has been the introduction of HYV seed. This ushered in the Green Revolution in the country. But the number of CSS has grown over the years and they have made deep inroads even into spheres falling within the domain of the States. There have been efforts from time to time for transferring the CSS to the States along with the corresponding funds, but not to much avail. A review undertaken by the Planning Commission showed that in 1995–96 there were 182 CSS under implementation with the Central funding of the order of Rs. 16,000 crores. This level of Central funding is even more than the normal Plan assistance given to the States for the State Plans. In principle, the CSS should be confined to schemes of an inter-State character, matters impinging on national security, selected national priorities where the central provision is essential for effective implementation, externally financed multi-State projects where the Central co-ordination is necessary for operational reasons and schemes necessitated by judicial intervention. Except for such schemes, all other schemes should be transferred to the States along with the corresponding funds. A detailed exercise has been done by the Planning Commission to identify the schemes, which could be transferred to the States in the light of the above approach. The CSS have been classified into the following four categories:

i. Those that may be retained for the reasons mentioned above;
ii. Those which are to be transferred with resources to be pooled and distributed among the States as per the Gadgil Formula;
iii. Those which are to be transferred with the earmarking of funds; and
iv. Those which are to be transferred in a phased manner.

A final decision in the matter would be taken, after ascertaining the views of the State Governments/Central Ministries, with the approval of the NDC. It is expected that it would be possible to transfer CSS with Central assistance of the order of Rs. 12,000 crores per annum (in terms of 1996–97 outlays) to the States over a period of time in a phased manner. While transferring the CSS to the States, it should be ensured that funds are earmarked for the PRIs /the ULBs in respect of schemes falling within the purview of the Eleventh and Twelfth Schedules of the Constitution.

The Planning Commission circulated a Note on Transfer of

Centrally Sponsored Schemes, in 1998, to all State Governments/ Union Territories for eliciting their comments. As the States/UTs expressed divergent views on the identification of schemes to be transferred and other related modalities, the Planning Commission prepared a Note on Transfer of Centrally Sponsored Schemes (CSS), as Agenda Item No. 5 submitted to the meeting of the National Development Council, held on 19 February 1999, Appendix 5.2. This Note included a list of all 184 Centrally Sponsored Schemes being implemented by various Central Ministries/Departments (as on 15 January 1999), for the consideration of the NDC for selection of schemes to be transferred. The modalities for transfer including selection of the schemes to be transferred, earmarking of funds and the time schedule for the transfer were also to be decided by the NDC. The Agenda Note also stated:

With respect to schemes which are transferred to the States/UTs, there should be complete flexibility for the States/UTs to continue, modify or even discontinue the schemes. For those schemes which are identified for transfer with earmarking of funds, the earmarking should be within the broad sectoral areas and flexibility should be given to the States to design the programmes/schemes as per their needs and priorities. In this case, there should be a process of joint plan formulation and joint monitoring between concerned Central Ministries/Departments, Planning Commission and State/UT Governments. Further, in the case of schemes falling within the purview of the Panchayati Raj Institutions (PRIS)/Urban Local Bodies (ULBS) as per the Eleventh and Twelfth Schedules of the 73rd and 74th Constitutional Amendment Acts, the transfer should be accompanied with earmarking of funds. Such schemes, along with corresponding State Plan schemes, need to be identified for transfer to the appropriate levels of Panchayats together with staff, functions and powers. In order to avoid future proliferation of Centrally Sponsored Schemes, new schemes should be introduced only in exceptional cases and with the approval of the full Planning Commission.

The following is an extract from the Minutes of the meeting of the NDC held on the 19 February 1999, relating to Agenda item No. 5.

5. The meeting noted that there is a wide divergence of opinion among the States and between the Central ministries and the States on the transfer

of Centrally Sponsored Schemes and the modalities of the transfer of the schemes. After discussions, the NDC decided to constitute a Sub-Committee of the NDC under the Chairmanship of the Deputy Chairman, Planning Commission, with a few Union Ministers and some State Chief Ministers as members.

And thus the charade of appointing committees, sub-committees, and working groups, goes on. The logical flaw in all these exercises is that the total limit on allocation of Central funds for the Centrally Sponsored Schemes is sought to be derived from the list of schemes finalized. The original exercise at the time of the Gadgil Formula first set a limit of 1/6 of total Central assistance for State Sector Plan and then specified what type of schemes could be formulated within this limit. What all needed now is to reiterate their limit and ask some Group to decide the schemes within that limit. Instead, each Committee or Group appointed so far had left the limit to be derived from an agreed list and one Committee even raised the limit to 1/3. Another Group opined that it might not be practicable to set any limit.

Where does this reluctance to reduce such schemes come from? After all, governments should be anxious to reduce their commitments outside their legitimate jurisdiction if this meant spending ones own funds. Basically the resistance comes from Central ministries dealing with subjects in the State List. These ministries have grown in size essentially on schemes implemented by the States. In the beginning, the role of ministries like the Agriculture Ministry did play a crucial role in achieving national goals like food self-sufficiency. A national policy on food distribution gave rise to the Ministry of Food. The same cannot, however, be said of ministries like Human Resource Development or subjects like cooperation. Had the task of reducing Centrally Sponsored Schemes been left to the Planning Commission or the Finance Ministry, a more rational review of the situation would have been possible. Now that the Plan revenue expenditure has also been referred to the Eleventh Finance Commission, a comprehensive review of Centrally Sponsored Schemes could even be referred to a Finance Commission.

The attitude of the States to Centrally Sponsored Schemes has not varied with political changes in State Governments. All parties when in power in the States have pressed for a reduction of Centrally Sponsored Schemes. At the Centre, however, non-Congress Governments have generally been more willing to take an objective view of this matter. The only time when a substantial cut in the allocation for the Centrally Sponsored Schemes was made and the resultant savings distributed to the States on the basis of the Gadgil Formula was when Dr. Lakdawala was the Deputy Chairman of the Planning Commission in 1979 and Morarji Desai was the Prime Minister.

APPENDIX 5.1

Summary of Recommendations of the Group of Officials

1. The Centrally Sponsored Schemes should be defined as the schemes which are funded directly by Central Ministries/Departments and implemented by the States or their agencies, irrespective of their pattern of financing, unless they fall under the Centre's sphere of responsibility i.e. the Union List. (para 14)
2. There should be no mid-plan introduction of schemes. In other words, all the schemes to be implemented in a given Plan period should have been included in the Five Year Plan. In exceptional cases, new schemes may be introduced to meet any emergent situation or to give effect to a new thrust in national policy (e.g. New Education Policy) but these should, as far as possible, be 100% Centrally funded. (para 15)
3. There should be prior consultation with the States, not administrative, but with Finance and Planning Departments, before introduction of new schemes and financial arrangements should be carefully worked out if the schemes are not 100% Centrally funded. In order that a broad view may be taken instead of a sectoral one by a particular Ministry, all new schemes should be approved by the full Planning Commission. (para 16)
4. The total number of Centrally Sponsored Schemes under implementation as on 1-4-1985 is 262. Excluding 24 schemes being implemented by autonomous bodies, the Group recommended the transfer of 113 schemes, involving a Seventh Plan outlay of Rs. 1260.72 crores, to the States. 125 schemes with a Seventh Plan outlay of Rs. 14,104.17 crores are to be retained. (para 21, Table)
5. All the retained schemes should be critically examined and evaluated with regard to their thrust and content before their inclusion in the Eighth Plan. This examination should be carried out by the Administrative Ministries/ Departments in consultation with the Ministry of Finance and the Planning Commission. (para 24)
6. States should have flexibility in the matter of implementation of schemes to enable them to achieve the objective of the scheme in a cost-effective manner keeping in view the special conditions and circumstances of each State. (para 25)
7. The transfer should be effective from the Eighth Plan. (para 27)
8. If transfer is desired from an earlier date, it could be from 1-4-1988 for remaining two years of the Seventh Plan. The updated figure of Rs. 800 crores available for 113 schemes to be transferred, could be distributed to the States according to the Modified Gadgil Formula. (para 27)

9. Central assistance to the States in respect of transferred schemes should be governed by the formula applicable for Central assistance to State Plans in the Eighth Plan period. The Special Category States should, however, continue to enjoy the special dispensation as heretofore. (para 29)
15. The Group felt that while it is necessary to limit Centrally Sponsored Schemes, both in terms of number and financial outlays, it might not be practical to lay down any ceiling.
16. A rigorous procedure of fulfilling the criteria proposed by the NDC Committee, prior consultation with the States and approval of the full Planning Commission should, however, ensure that the propensity for proliferation of schemes is kept in check. (para 32)
11. The schemes deleted/transferred to States should not be re-introduced in any other manner nor should other schemes expand to take their place. In other words, the transfer should result in proportionate reduction in the Central expenditure and net addition to the resources being transferred to the States. (para 33)
12. The Central Ministries should thoroughly look into the schemes being retained and if any scheme is likely to reach a stage where any component of it is likely to be transferred to the maintenance phase, thereby increasing the non-plan liability of the States, the Ninth Finance Commission should be notified of the same well in time. (para 34)
13. Central assistance to States in the Eighth Plan, by whatever formula it is determined, should take into account the additional requirements on account of the transferred schemes in case the transfer takes effect from the Eighth Plan. (para 35)

APPENDIX 5.2

Agenda Item No. 5: Transfer of Centrally Sponsored Schemes (CSS) (Submitted for the Meeting of the NDC held on 19-2-1999)

Centrally Sponsored Schemes (CSS) have been implemented from the beginning of the First Five Year Plan. Over the time the number of CSS have grown, and from time to time there have been attempts at transferring some of these to the States along with funds. At the time of discussion of the 'Approach to the Seventh Five Year Plan' this issue was raised again. An Expert Group under the Chairmanship of Shri K. Ramamurthy was set up to review this subject. The NDC, while considering the Ramamurthy Report in 1985, resolved that a Committee of the NDC be set up to examine the Report. Accordingly, a Committee was set up under Shri P.V. Narasimha Rao, the then Minister of Human Resources Development. This NDC Committee, in turn, constituted a group of officials under the then Secretary, Planning Commission, to work out the details regarding the retention of CSS, mode of transfer, etc. This Group recommended that out of 262 Centrally Sponsored Schemes, which were under implementation at the commencement of the Seventh Plan, 113 be transferred to States with resources.

1. At the National Development Council meeting held in January 1997, to discuss the Draft Approach to the Ninth Five Year Plan, several Chief Ministers opined that the CSS should be transferred to the States along with the resources, especially those falling within the purview of the State List as per the Constitution and retention of CSS be limited to those as identified by the Approach Paper to the Ninth Five Year Plan. On this issue, the Approach Paper states that, 'In principle, Centrally Sponsored Schemes should be confined to schemes of an inter-State character; matters impinging on national security; selected national priorities where Central supervision is essential for effective implementation; and multi-State externally financed projects where central co-ordination is necessary for operational reasons.' The Ninth Five Year Plan Document also reiterates the same.
2. Earlier, a Note on Transfer of Centrally Sponsored Schemes was circulated to all State Governments/UTs for eliciting their comments. The States/UTs have expressed divergent views on the identification of schemes to be transferred and other modalities. Therefore, a list of all CSS being implemented by various Central Ministries/Departments, may be considered by the NDC for selection of schemes to be transferred. The modalities for transfer including selection of the schemes to be transferred with the earmarking of funds and the time schedule

for the transfer also need to be decided by the NDC. With respect to schemes, which are transferred to the States/UTs, there should be complete flexibility for the States/UTs to continue, modify or even discontinue the schemes. For those schemes which are identified for transfer with earmarking of funds, the earmarking should be within the broad sectoral areas and flexibility should be given to the States/UTs to design the programmes/schemes as per their needs and priorities. In this case, there should be a process of joint plan formulation and joint monitoring between the concerned Central Ministries/Departments, Planning Commission and State/UT Governments. Further, in the case of schemes falling within the purview of Panchayati Raj Institutions (PRI)/Urban Local Bodies as per the Eleventh and Twelfth Schedules of the 73rd and 74th Constitutional Amendment Acts, the transfer should be accompanied with earmarking of funds to local bodies. Such schemes along with corresponding State Plan schemes need to be identified for transfer to the appropriate level of Panchayats together with staff, functions and powers.

3. In order to avoid future proliferation of Centrally Sponsored Schemes, new schemes should be introduced only in exceptional cases and with the approval of the full Planning Commission.

List of Centrally Sponsored Schemes (CSS) (As on 15 January 1999)

Department of Agriculture and Cooperation: Ministry of Agriculture

1. Assistance to Cooperatives of Weaker Sections
2. Assistance to Women's Cooperatives
3. Integrated Water-shed Development in Flood-prone Rivers
4. Reclamation of Alkali (Usar) Soils
5. Oil seeds Production Programme
6. National Pulses Development Programme
7. Oil Palm Development Programme
8. National Watershed Development Programme for Rain-fed Areas
9. Improvement of Crop Statistics (ICS)
10. Timely Reporting of Estimates of Area and Production of Principal Crops
11. Livestock Census
12. Accelerated Maize Development Programme
13. Assistance to Cooperative Credit Institutions in Under-developed States and Special Areas (Non Over Due Cover)
14. Agricultural Credit Stabilisation Fund
15. Assistance to Cooperative Marketing, Processing and Storage in Under-developed States and Union Territories
16. Share Capital Participation in Cooperative Sugar Factories
17. Share Capital Participation in Cooperative Spinning Mills (Growers)
18. Establishment of an Agency for Reporting of Agricultural Statistics (ERAS)
19. Crop Estimation Survey on Fruits, Vegetables and Minor Crops
20. Technology Mission for Cotton Development
21. Integrated Cereals Development Programme in Rice Based Cropping System Areas (ICDP—Rice)
22. Integrated Cereals Development Programme in Wheat Based Cropping System Areas (ICDP—Wheat)
23. Integrated Cereals Development Programme in Coarse Cereals Based Cropping System Areas (ICDP—Coarse Cereals)
24. Special Jute Development Programme
25. Intensive Cotton Development Programme
26. Sustainable Development of Sugarcane Based Cropping System
27. Balanced and Integrated Use of Fertilisers
28. Promotion of Agricultural Mechanisation among Small Farmers
29. Integrated Programme for Development of Spices
30. Integrated Development of Cashew-nut
31. Use of Plastics in Agriculture
32. Soil Conservation in Catchments of River Valley Projects
33. Special Scheme for Scheduled Castes (SCs) and Scheduled Tribes (STs)

Department of Animal Husbandry and Dairying: Ministry of Agriculture

34. Progeny Testing Programme
35. Assistance to States for Feed and Fodder Development
36. Professional Efficiency Development
37. National Bull Production Programme
38. National Ram/Buck Development Programme
39. Development and Preservation of Pack Animals
40. Assistance to States for Integrated Piggery Development
41. Freshwater Aqua Culture
42. Fish Harbour Facilities at Minor Ports
45. Welfare of Fishermen
46. Extension of Frozen Technology
47. Improvement of Slaughter Houses
48. Establishment of Carcass Utilisation Centres/Flaying Units
49. National Project on Rinderpest Eradication
50. Systematic Control of Animal Diseases
51. Foot and Mouth Diseases
52. Animal Disease Surveillance
53. Integrated Sample Surveys for Estimation of Major Livestock Products

Department of Education: Ministry of Human Resources Development

54. Environment Orientation to School Children
55. Improvement of Science Education in Schools
56. Assistance to NGOs for Strengthening of Hostel Facilities for Girls
57. Integrated Education for Disabled Children
58. Rural Functional Literacy Project
59. Computer Education in Schools
60. Vocationalization of Education
61. Promotion of Yoga
62. Education Technology
62. Strengthening of Administrative Structure
63. Appointment of Hindi Teachers
65. (a) Post Literacy and Continuing Education
    (b) Special Programme for Eradication of Illiteracy
66. Appointment of Urdu Teachers
67. Operation Black Board
68. Teacher Education
69. Non-formal Education (Elementary)
70. Nutritional Support to Primary education (Midday Meal)

Department of Family Welfare: Ministry of Health and Family Welfare

71. National Family Welfare Programme

Department of Food and Civil Supplies: Ministry of Food and Consumer Affairs

72. Purchase of Mobile Vans/Trucks
73. Construction of Godowns

Department of Health: Ministry of Health and Family Welfare

74. National Malaria Eradication Programme
75. National Leprosy Eradication Programme
76. National TB Eradication Programme
77. National Programme of Prevention of Blindness
78. National AIDS Control Programme
79. Assistance for augmentation of Drug Testing Facilities in States so.
80. Drug Inspectorate Staff in various States and Union Territories
81. Financial Assistance to States for Strengthening Food Testing Laboratories
82. Assistance for Upgradation of Postgraduates
83. National Guinea-Worm Eradication Programme

Department of Industrial Policy and Promotion: Ministry of Industry

84. Growth Centres Scheme
85. Transport Subsidy Scheme

Department of Justice: Ministry of Law and Justice and Company Affairs

86. Development of Infra-structural facilities for the Judiciary

Department of Revenue: Ministry of Finance

87. Setting up of Special Courts for Trial of Offences under the Narcotic Drugs and Psychotropic Substances Act, 1985 (NDPS)

Department of Sports and Youth Affairs: Ministry of Human Resources Development

88. Establishment and Development of Mountaineering Institutes
89. National Service Scheme
90. Games and Sports in Colleges and Universities

Department of Women and Child Development: Ministry of Human Resources Development

91. Indira Mahila Yojana
92. Integrated Child Development Scheme (ICDS)
93. World Bank assisted ICDS Schemes
94. Rural women's Development and Employment Project

Ministry of Commerce

95. Export Promotion Industrial Parks

Ministry of Environment and Forests

96. Seed Development Agencies
97. Paryavaran Sudhar Yojana—Environment Improvement and Dissemination Scheme
98. Fuel Wood/Fodder Project
99. Aerial Seeding
100. Non-timber Forest Produce including Medicinal Plants
101. Promotion of Construction of Common Effluent Treatment Plants (CETP) for clusters of Small Scale Industrial Units
102. Industrial Pollution Control Projects
103. Biosphere Reserves
104. Conservation and Management of Mangroves
105. Conservation and Management of Wet-lands
106. Ganga Action Plan—Phase I
107. Ganga Action Plan—Phase II
108. National River Action Plan
109. Association of Scheduled Tribes and Rural Poor in Regeneration of Degraded Forests
110. Introduction of Modern Fire Control Methods
111. Development of National Parks and Sanctuaries
112. Project Tiger
113. Beneficiary-Oriented Scheme for Tribal Development
114. Eco-development around Sanctuaries and National Parks including Tiger Reserves
115. Project Elephant
116. Integrated Afforestation and Eco-Development Project
117. Taj Protection Mission

Ministry of Labour

118. World Bank Aided schemes
119. Rehabilitation of Bonded Labour

Ministry of Non-conventional Energy Sources

120. National Programme on Improved Chulha
121. Institutional/Community Bio-Gas Development
122. Integrated Rural Energy Programme
123. National project on Bio-Gas Development
124. Solar Photo-Voltaic Lantern/Domestic Lighting Programme
125. Small Hydro-Power Programme

Ministry of Power

126. Inter-State Transmission

Ministry of Rural Areas and Employment

127. Rural Water Supply Programme
128. Rural Sanitation
129. Jawahar Rozgar Yojana
130. Employment Assurance Scheme
131. Indira Awaas Yojana
132. Strengthening of State Training Centre
133. Strengthening of Extension Training Centre
134. Roads in Special Problem Areas
135. National Social Assistance Programme
136. Million Wells Programme
137. Drought Prone Areas Programme
138. Desert Development Programme
139. Computerisation of Land Records
140. Strengthening of Revenue Administration and Updating of Land Records
141. Integrated Rural Development Programme
142. Training of Rural Youth for Self-employment
143. Development of Women and Children in Rural Areas
144. District Rural Development Agencies (DRDA) Administration

Ministry of Social Justice and Empowerment

145. Scheduled Castes Development Corporation
146. Boys Hostels for SCs
147. Girls Hostels for SCs
148. Book Banks for SC/ST Students
149. Coaching and Allied Schemes
150. Post-Matric Scholarships to SC/ST Students
151. Pre-Matric Scholarships for Children of those engaged in Unclean Occupations
152. Girls Hostels for STs
153. Boys Hostels for STs
154. Ashram Schools for STs
155. Grants to Tribal Research Institutes and Award of Research Fellowships
156. National Scheme of Liberation and Rehabilitation of Scavengers
157. Implementation of Protection of Civil Rights Act, 1965 and SC/ST (Prevention of Atrocities) Act, 1989
158. Employment of Handicapped
159. National Programme for Rehabilitation of the Disabled
160. Scheme for Prevention and Control of Juvenile Social Maladjustment
161. Post-Matric Scholarships for OBCs
162. Pre-Matric Scholarships for OBCs
163. Hostels for OBC Boy and Girl Students
164. Residential Schools for OBC Boy and Girl Students

Ministry of Surface Transport

165. Economic and Inter-State Importance (E&I)
    (a) Inter-State Roads and Bridges
    (b) Roads and Bridges of Economic Importance
166. Inland Water Transportation Schemes Implemented by States

Ministry of Textiles

167. Scheme for Handloom Exports
168. Project Package—All States and North East
169. Handloom Development Centre/Quality Dyeing Unit
170. Welfare Schemes, Work Shed-cum-Housing
171. Group Insurance
172. Thrift Fund
173. Loans to State Governments (for Handloom Weavers)—North-East

Ministry of Urban Affairs and Employment

174. Urban Low Cost Sanitation Scheme for Liberation of Scavengers
175. Accelerated Urban Water Supply Programme for Towns with population of less than 20,000
176. Integrated Development of Small and Medium Towns
177. Mega City Scheme
178. Contribution to National Capital Region Planning Board
179. Contribution to Urban Transport Consortium Fund
180. Swarna Jayanti Shaheri Rozgar Yojana

Ministry of Water Resources

181. Command Area Development Programme
182. Central Loan Assistance to Government of Assam
183. Rationalization of Minor Irrigation Statistics

Planning Commission

184. Strengthening of Planning Machinery at State and District Level

6

Modifications and Revisions to the Gadgil Formula

FIFTH FIVE YEAR PLAN: 1974–1979

The formulation of criteria for allocation of Central assistance among States for the Fifth Plan period was to be taken up along with the finalization of the Fifth Five Year Plan. For various reasons this could not be done at the time of commencement of the Fifth Plan. In view of this, an *ad hoc* decision was taken by the Planning Commission to maintain Central assistance for the Annual Plan for 1974–5 at the same level as for 1973–4, the last year of the Fourth Plan, i.e. at Rs. 755.15 crores. During the year, as per the recommendations of the Sixth Finance Commission, an amount of Rs. 50 crores was given as advance plan assistance for relief works in States affected by natural calamities. Jammu & Kashmir received an advance assistance of Rs. 29 crores to fill the gap in resources that remained even after the recommendations of the Finance Commission.

The same procedure was continued in 1975–6 as well. An amount of Rs. 35 crores was given to States affected by natural calamities and an advance assistance of Rs. 239 crores was also given to cover gaps in resources of certain States to enable them to meet inescapable requirements, or accelerate the execution of selected irrigation and power projects. An assistance of Rs. 6 crores was given to Sikkim, which became a State in the Indian Union.

For 1976–7, normal assistance (which was being given at 1973–4 level) was stepped up by 10 per cent over 1973–4 level and a provision of Rs. 231 crores was made for advance plan assistance.

Together with the finalization of the Fifth Five Year Plan, consideration of a formula for allocation of Central assistance to States was undertaken in July–August 1976. There were two options before the Planning Commission: (1) to re-examine the Gadgil

Formula, or (2) to apply the existing Gadgil Formula for the Fifth Plan period also, with such modifications as may be necessary. It was decided that consistent with the approach adopted in the past years, it would be both desirable and least controversial if the Gadgil Formula was *updated and adopted* for the Fifth Plan period as a whole. Exercises were made on the basis of updated data under different criteria of the Gadgil Formula, which were considered by the National Development Council in its meeting held in September 1976.

Under the original Gadgil Formula, 10 per cent of the total assistance for States (excluding Assam, Jammu & Kashmir, and Nagaland) was allocated on the basis of 'Special Problems' of States which, at that time, were illustrated as drought-affected, hill, tribal, metropolitan, and desert areas. All these problems, except for desert areas, were subsequently taken care of by separate programmes under the Fifth Plan and could not be said to constitute special problems of a few States to form a basis, once again, for special assistance within the Formula. On the other hand, financing a minimum necessary Plan outlay had itself become a problem in the case of some States. The Plan outlays of States were fixed, taking into account priorities and programmes considered equally desirable in the National/ Regional/ State interests. If, having done so, it was found that even after taking into account the best efforts of the State to raise its own resources and the dispensation of the Finance Commission and Central assistance as entitled to under the Gadgil Formula, a State was not in a position to finance such a Plan outlay, then it was felt that such a State should be considered a 'problem State'.

Consequently an updated Gadgil Formula was approved by the NDC as follows:

Fifth Five Year Plan: 1974–1979

1. Population:	60 per cent	On the basis of 1971 census figures.
2. Per capita State income:	10 per cent	Only to those States whose per capita income is below the

		national average. Average per capita SDP was worked out at current prices for three years 1970–3, as finalized by the Central Statistical Organization.
3. Tax effort:	10 per cent	State tax receipts for 1973–4 in relation to per capita State Income as under point 2.
4. Irrigation and power projects:	10 per cent	Revised Fifth Plan outlays on continuing major irrigation and power schemes, each with an estimated cost of Rs. 20 crores and above and expenditure of at least 10 per cent by the end of 1973–4.
5. Special problems:	10 per cent	To cover gaps in resources for financing the inescapable outlays in core sectors of the Plan, as well as allocation for desert areas of Gujarat, Haryana, and Rajasthan.

An amount of Rs. 20 crores was distributed among Gujarat, Haryana and Rajasthan for desert areas while the balance amount under the criterion of 'Special Problems' was distributed among States having gaps in resources as explained above.

For the Fifth Plan as a whole, the total Central assistance was taken at Rs. 6,000 crores. Out of this, Rs. 450 crores was allocated for hill and tribal areas and the North-East States. Central assistance for plan schemes assisted under IDA/World Bank aid was hitherto taken as part of the total entitlement under the Gadgil Formula. In essence, therefore, such dispensation was assistance to the Central Government and not additional assistance for the State concerned. This led to a lack of interest on the part of the States to pose schemes for such external assistance or for drawing such assistance expeditiously once it was sanctioned. It was, therefore, considered desirable to give extra Central assistance to the extent of 15 to 20 per cent of IDA/World Bank disbursements with respect to such State Plan projects. A sum of Rs. 100 crores was reserved for providing extra assistance to the States in respect of Plan schemes financed by IDA/World Bank assistance. The remaining amount of Rs. 5,450 crores was proposed to be allocated among the States on the basis of the Updated Gadgil Formula.

It would be recalled that a lump sum allocation had been made for Assam, Jammu & Kashmir and Nagaland under the Gadgil Formula. Himachal Pradesh, other North-Eastern Council States and Sikkim had since became States. It was, therefore, decided that the lump sum provision under the Gadgil Formula for the Fifth Plan period would cover these States as well. An amount of Rs. 1,150 crores was set apart for this purpose. The balance amount of Rs. 4,300 crores was distributed among the remaining States on the basis of updated calculations in terms of the Gadgil Formula. Advance Plan assistance given to States in the earlier years was to be adjusted in the total entitlement worked out for them for the Fifth Plan period as a whole, in order to arrive at the amount to be allocated for the last two years (1977–8 and 1978–9) of the Plan period.

In March 1977, the first non-Congress Government at the Centre (under Morarji Desai) decided to terminate the Fifth Five Year Plan with the 1977–8 Annual Plan and commence the Sixth Five Year Plan for 1978–83 with the 'Rolling Plan' concept. The imminent report of the Seventh Finance Commission, the advent of a new Five Year Plan and the emergence of governments belonging to different political parties in various States gave rise to an intense debate on Centre-State financial relations. In this context, there was demand for a re-examination of the existing formula and the procedure adopted for allocation of Central assistance for State Plans.

The National Development Council, at its meeting held on 18 and 19 March 1977, resolved that a Committee should be formed to discuss fiscal arrangements in the light of the Draft Five Year Plan 1978–83, which would, *inter alia*, review the Gadgil Formula and the scope of Centrally Sponsored Schemes. A Committee was constituted with Deputy Chairman Planning Commission (P.N. Haksar), as the Chairman and Chief Ministers of all States as Members.

The first meeting of the NDC Committee was held on 21 August 1978. (D.T. Lakdawala was the Deputy Chairman of the Planning Commission by that time—June 1977 to February 1980.) All the Chief Ministers of States presented their views on the Gadgil Formula and the Committee appointed a Working Group to examine in detail the questions involved and report back to the Committee. The Working Group held three meetings and discussed the issues at length but could not come to any definite conclusion on a formula for allocation of Central assistance to States. The NDC Committee met on 19 and 20 January 1979 to consider the views of the Chief Ministers on an alternative formula suggested by the Deputy Chairman (D.T. Lakdawala), Planning Commission, in a paper submitted to the Working Group at its meeting held on 10 and 11 January 1979.

There was a sharp division of opinion in regard to the Gadgil Formula, with six States wanting it to be continued and eight States wanting some alternative formula. The Deputy Chairman, Planning Commission, then put forward a compromise formula and it was agreed to, under which the Gadgil Formula would continue to apply to the distribution of Rs. 4, 200 crores among 14 States (other than the special category States) for 1979–83. This amount of Rs. 4,200 crores was worked out as in Table 6.1:

TABLE 6.1: TOTAL ASSISTANCE TO BE MADE AVAILABLE UNDER GADGIL FORMULA FOR 1979–83

(*Rs. crores*)

(i)	Aggregate Central assistance proposed for five years 1978–83	10,350
(ii)	Less—amount already allocated in 1978–9	(-) 2,450
(iii)	Amount available for four years 1979–83	7,900
(iv)	Less—amount for Special Category States	(-) 1,800
(v)	Less—amount for Hill and Tribal Areas and North-East Council	(-) 800
(vi)	Less—amount for externally aided projects	(-) 500
(vii)	Less—reserve for special problems	(-) 600
(viii)	Amount available for four years 1979–83 under the Gadgil Formula	4,200

Source: Agenda papers submitted to the meeting of the NDC on 19-3-1979.

For the amount of Rs. 2,000 crores that was to be available through reduction in the outlays for Centrally Sponsored Schemes, the Deputy Chairman proposed that it be distributed on the basis of the '*inverse of per capita income multiplied by population*', i.e. IATP (Income Adjusted Total Population), which is a more objective formula as compared to other alternatives suggested. The Prime Minister, Morarji Desai, as Chairman of the National Development Council, announced his decision in the meeting of the National Development Council held on 19 March 1979. Relevant extracts from the summary record of this meeting are:

86. . . . The Centre had agreed to give Rs. 2,000 crores obtained by implementing the report submitted by Secretary, planning Commission for distribution among the States. There was, however, no agreement about its distribution among States. There was a suggestion that Rs. 2,000 crores might be distributed for the Antyodaya schemes, but it was found that there was no agreement about it. The formula which had now been devised was called IATP. He confessed that he did not understand the jargon. However, he found that it worked out in a satisfactory manner. According to this formula, Rs. 2,000 crores would be distributed like this: Andhra Pradesh—Rs.161 crores; Bihar—Rs. 300 crores; Gujarat—Rs. 81 crores; Haryana—Rs. 25 crores; Karnataka—Rs. 96 crores; Kerala—Rs. 77 crores; Madhya Pradesh—Rs. 184 crores; Maharashtra—Rs. 128 crores; Orissa—Rs. 95 crores; Punjab—Rs. 29 crores; Rajasthan—Rs. 103 crores; Tamil Nadu—Rs. 150 crores; Uttar Pradesh—Rs. 424 crores; and West Bengal—Rs. 147 crores.

88. The Prime Minister assured the special category States that funds would be made available to them outside Rs. 2,000 crores for their proper share in the Centrally Sponsored Schemes. He said that Rs. 4,200 crores would be distributed according to Gadgil Formula because in spite of all the discussions for months it was not possible to devise any other arrangement.

As already mentioned, in the Updated Gadgil Formula, 10 per cent of the assistance was allocated for special problems and not according to the general objective criteria. However, it was now decided that while 90 per cent of the amount would continue to be distributed on the basis of the criteria mentioned above, the balance of 10 per cent would also be distributed in the same proportion as worked out for the 90 per cent component. This method was continued to be referred to as the Updated Gadgil Formula, as it is only slightly different from its earlier version.

SIXTH FIVE YEAR PLAN: 1980–1985

There was a change of government at the Centre in January 1980 and as such the Rolling Plan concept, introduced by the first non-Congress Government at the Centre, was limited to the Annual Plans for 1978–9 and 1979–80. In the event, the rolling plan concept was never implemented and the Plans for 1978–9 and 1979–80 were treated as Annual Plans as previously. The new Government (under Prime Minister Indira Gandhi) reverted to the Five Year Plan concept and the Sixth Five Year Plan came into effect for the period 1980–5. The Gadgil Formula once again came in for further review.

The thirty-fourth meeting of the National Development Council, held on 30 and 31 August 1980 discussed 'Sixth Five Year Plan—A Framework', and also the formula for distribution of Central assistance to States. Some relevant extracts from the Summary Record of this meeting are given below:

> The Deputy Chairman concluded by saying that the new Plan sought the national consensus through the NDC, whereas the Rolling Plan of the previous Government did not even have the approval of the then Government. Planning being a continuous process, plan documents would necessarily repeat some of the projects and programmes. The most important factor was that the *status quo ante* of the planning process started by Shri Jawaharlal Nehru had been restored.
>
> The Prime Minister, Smt. Indira Gandhi observed that the deliberations at the Council's meeting reminded us of the task before us. Every State considered itself backward but some States were more backward than others were, and she desired that those, which were less backward, should keep this in mind.
>
> The Prime Minister observed that the basic objectives of the Plan remained the same, as before. Emphasis on certain matters had been placed in the Approach Paper because these were completely neglected in the previous Draft. In regard to Centrally Sponsored Schemes, particularly those schemes, which had been transferred to the States, she stated that they need

a fresh examination, as most States had either not used the funds fully or had not used them at all, e.g. soil conservation in river valleys, social forestry and farm forestry, formations of manurial composting, subsidy for improved and quality seeds and inter-State transmission lines. The Bihar Chief Minister also mentioned the police-housing scheme.

Referring to the Gadgil Formula, the Prime Minister stated that there was no formula which could satisfy every State. *She, however, announced that the 10 per cent allocation under the Gadgil Formula for continuing schemes started in the Fourth plan and continued in the three Annual Plans, which was an ad hoc agreement, could now be transferred to the States whose per capita income was less than the national average. She suggested that this could be done by the Planning Commission itself rather than having a committee on the subject. She also announced that a part of the market borrowings could be allocated to the backward States whose per capita income and plan outlay were below the national average.* (Italics as in the Summary Record)

With this increase in the per capita income criterion to 20 per cent, the Gadgil Formula was called the Modified Gadgil Formula.

According to the above decision taken at the thirty-fourth meeting of the NDC held in August 1980, details of the Modified Gadgil Formula were as under:

1. A lump sum is to be set apart for meeting the requirements of eight Special Category States, viz., Assam, Himachal Pradesh, Jammu & Kashmir, Manipur, Meghalaya, Tripura and Sikkim, out of the total pool of Central assistance.
2. The balance of Central assistance is to be distributed among the remaining 14 States on the basis of

(a) 60 per cent:	on the basis of population according to 1971 census.
(b) 10 per cent:	on the basis of tax effort—per capita State tax receipts as a proportion of per capita SDP for 1973–6.
(c) 20 per cent:	on the basis of average per capita SDP for 1973–6—only to those States whose per capita SDP is below the national average.
(d) 10 per cent:	on the basis of special problems.

The Gadgil Formula as revised by the Janata Government in 1979 and the Modified Gadgil Formula as finalized by the Congress Government in 1980 as part of the deliberations on the Sixth Five Year Plan 1980–5, are:

(i) 10 per cent allocated under 'continuing irrigation and power projects' in the original Gadgil Formula and continued in the Updated Gadgil Formula in 1979, was added to the 'per capita income' criterion in 1980 to make it 20 per cent.

(ii) 10 per cent under 'special problems' remained the same in both the formulae, but the content was different. The amount under this criterion in the 1979 formula was to be distributed to States in the same proportion as of the 90 per cent assistance. In the modification of 1980, this amount was again meant to be allocated for 'special problems' of States only.

In the Sixth Five Year Plan (1980–5) Central assistance aggregating to Rs. 15,350 crores was allocated to States as per the following details:

(*Rs. crores*)

1.	Total Central assistance		15,350
2	Area Programmes		
	(a) Hill Areas	560	
	(b) Tribal Areas	470	
	(c) North East Council	325	
	(d) Externally Aided Schemes	1,450	
	Total of 2		2,805
3.	Balance (1–2)		12,545
4.	Amount set apart for 8 Special Category States		3,245
5.	Amount set apart for distribution under IATP Formula (out of Rs. 2,000 crores envisaged in the Plan for 1978–83, as saving out of transfer of certain Centrally Sponsored Schemes)		1,600
6.	Balance available for distribution among 14 non-Special Category States under the Modified Gadgil Formula		7,700

SEVENTH FIVE YEAR PLAN: 1985–1990

The Seventh Five Year Plan (1985–90) was to commence from 1985–6 and the National Development Council, in its meeting held on 8 and 9 November 1985, considered the Draft Seventh Plan

Document. Deputy Chairman, Planning Commission (Dr. Manmohan Singh) made the following observations as regards Central assistance.

225. Replying to the points made on the future of Gadgil Formula, the Deputy Chairman said that the Commission had noted all the view points raised. The Gadgil Formula represented a compromise arrived at with great difficulty. However, this was not the last word. The Commission would examine various suggestions for modifying the formula. Once the Commission was ready with some concrete ideas, these would be placed before the NDC and its guidance sought. He thanked all the Chief Ministers for the support and the confidence that they had shown in the Planning Commission. (Summary Record of the proceedings)

The Modified Gadgil Formula was continued for the Seventh Plan as well. The Central assistance allocated for the States' Seventh Plan was as under:

(Rs. crores)

1. Total Central assistance	29,886
2. Area Programmes	
(a) Hill Areas	870
(b) Tribal Areas	756
(c) North-East Council	575
(d) Border Areas	200
(e) Others	58
Total of 2	2,459
3. Balance (1–2)	27,427
Allocated for:	
i. Externally Aided Projects	3,800
ii. Special category States	7,102
iii. Non-Special Category States under the Modified Gadgil Formula	16,525
4. Deduct—Adjustments for advance plan assistance for relief works.	(–) 149
5. Net Central Assistance for State Plans (1–4)	29,737

Source: Seventh Plan Document.

TWO ANNUAL PLANS: 1990–1992

There was a change of Government at the Centre in December 1989 and the National Front came to power. They prepared the 'Approach to the Eighth Five Year Plan', which was considered in the forty-first meeting of the National Development Council, held on 18 and 19 June 1990. The following extract from the Summary Record of the NDC meeting has a bearing on the issue of Central assistance.

194. Shri Hegde (Deputy Chairman, Planning Commission) mentioned that several issues had been raised. He did not want to either reply to those issues or even mention all of them one-by-one because it would take some time. Prime Minister would deal with several points that had been raised. But one of the points he might refer to by way of clarification was that the Gadgil formula was not the *Gita* or the Bible. We have had first the Gadgil Formula several years ago and later on the Modified Gadgil Formula. As the situation had changed, it would be necessary to make changes in the formula also. Therefore, they were going to consider the suggestions made and see the kind of weightage that had to be given so that the disparity between region and region could be minimised.

Here we may go back a little to follow the thread of discussion. It will be recalled that the then Deputy Chairman, Planning Commission (Dr. Manmohan Singh), stated in the meeting of the NDC held in November 1985 that, 'the Commission would examine various suggestions for modifying the formula. Once the Commission was ready with some concrete ideas, these would be placed before the NDC and its guidance sought.' The need for such a revision, consistent with the objectives laid down in the Approach Paper on the Eighth Plan was also reiterated by the Deputy Chairman, Planning Commission (Ramakrishna Hegde), in the NDC meeting held on 18 and 19 June 1990 quoted earlier.

The Planning Commission prepared, in connection with the formulation of the Eighth Five Year Plan (1990–5), a paper on 'Distribution of Central Budget Support for States' Plan Expenditure', which is reproduced in fuli in Appendix 6.1. We quote here some relevant portions from this Paper.

Reduction in regional disparities and improvement in the quality of life, are two main goals to be kept in view while considering the issues connected with the transfer of funds from Centre to States. Therefore, the revision of the Modified Gadgil Formula has to be taken up keeping these objectives in sharp focus. At the same time, the basic soundness of the Formula as well as the fact that its core has stood the test of time, should not be ignored. It is also desirable to avoid drastic reduction in the share of assistance to any State as a result of the proposed revision. Hence, the revision now proposed, while seeking to help the weaker States, has to be of modest dimension. With due regard to these considerations, certain specific aspects of the existing formula have been identified for attempting corrections. They are briefly mentioned below.

(i) *Population* vs. *Area*

At present 60 per cent weight goes to population. A high weight to this factor is obviously justified. However, it is time to recognise the special problems relevant to States with large areas and low density of population. A small weight of, say, 5 per cent for area can be considered. 1971 population will continue to be the basis for applying the population factor.

(ii) *Backwardness*

The original Gadgil Formula gave this factor a weight of 10 per cent. The Modified Gadgil Formula, now in vogue, has given 20 per cent weight to this factor. Obviously, this is meant to help the relatively weaker States. Whether this weight could be further increased or not, is an aspect for consideration. If an enhancement is called for, should the benefit be given only to those States whose per capita income is below the national average or should the enhanced part benefit all States in relation to their respective distances from the highest income State? The emphasis in the Approach Document on removal of disparities would imply preference for the former.

(iii) *Tax Effort*

Presently, 10 per cent weight is given for tax effort. Unweighted tax ratio is the basis for distribution of this part of the assistance. Experience over the years has clearly demonstrated that tax effort, by itself, is not a correct indicator of State's fiscal management. A State, which attains a high level of taxation may, by having an unusually high level of non-plan expenditure, neutralise that advantage as far as Plan is concerned. So, it seems better to replace the factor of tax effort by one covering total fiscal management. The best way to measure this seems to be to assess the difference between the State's own total plan resources, estimated at the time of finalising the annual plans, and their actual performance. Those who do relatively better, in comparison with their own promise, would get a higher proportion of this part of assistance. To begin with, the assessment could be based on

1985–90 performance to be annually updated when data for subsequent years become available.

(iv) *Social Indicators*

The present formula gives no special consideration for attaining a higher level of performance in the factors that determine the quality of life. Nor is there any incentive for rapid improvement in States, which lag behind in this respect. All the Chief Ministers have expressed concern about the growth in population, which is a major hurdle in the efforts to improve the quality of life of our people. It is, therefore, proposed to give some weight to the factor of quality of life, so as to reward past achievements and to spur better performance in future. As an appropriate data base is not yet available, Infant Mortality Rate, measured by Sample Registration System, is proposed to be used, as first proxy for distributing 5 per cent of the assistance under the Formula for the Eighth Plan. A part of the amount will be distributed in proportion to the past achievement and the other part in proportion to the targets for future achievement. Each State's entitlement will be reviewed and re-fixed every year, taking into account its actual performance against the targets.

(v) *Special Problems*

This component, presently with a weight of 10 per cent, has been operated on an essentially discretionary basis. It is proposed to specify the types of purposes/problems for which this part of the assistance could be used. An illustrative list is given below:

Special Area Programmes (other than North-East Council)

Other special development problems such as Hill areas, Tribal areas, Border areas, flood/desert/drought-prone areas, Urban slums, Coastal areas, Special environmental issues, Special financial difficulties (that threaten achievement of a minimum plan size in particular States), included in a list to be approved by the NDC.

Upward adjustment is proposed to be made to ensure that the reduction in share of some States resulting from the above mentioned revision of the Modified Gadgil Formula for distributing Central assistance is contained within a reasonable level, say 7 per cent of their respective shares under the existing Modified Gadgil Formula. This could, if necessary, be treated as the charge on the total Central assistance for the Eighth Plan.

Variants to the Existing Formula

Keeping in view the aspects brought out in the foregoing paragraphs, a few alternatives of an illustrative type are indicated below:

	Population	*Area*	*Per capita income*	*Social indicator*	*T E/ FM*	*Spl Prob.*
Existing formula	60	–	20	–	10 (TE)	10
Alternative I	50	5	25	5	5 (FM)	10
Alternative II	50	–	25	5	5 (FM)	15
Alternative III	55	–	20	5	5 (FM)	15
Alternative IV	55	–	25	–	10 (FM)	10
Alternative V	55	–	20	–	10 (FM)	15

TE = Tax Effort FM = Fiscal Management

As stated earlier, in the initial allocation for the Eighth Plan no State need suffer a reduction in share of more than 7 per cent compared to the position as per the formula now in vogue. Even this limited reduction (not exceeding 7 per cent) may, to some extent, be made up by the expansion of the coverage of the formula-based assistance by adding to it amounts which, under the existing formula, are set apart for Special Area Programmes. However, if the annual review of performance in respect of the factors of Social Indicator and Fiscal Management and the consequent re-fixation of assistance result in larger reduction, the States concerned will have to accept it as the direct result of their actual performance. On the other hand, States can look forward to improved share of assistance if they can improve their performance under Social Indicator and Fiscal Management.

Some other modifications are also proposed in the existing system of distribution of Central assistance. These relate mainly to the enhancement of States' share in external aid for projects implemented as part of State Plans, some limit-fixation in the proportion of Central assistance going to Special Category States, and inclusion of a substantial part of the funds for Centrally Sponsored Schemes as part of block assistance to be automatically released to States on monthly/quarterly basis.

The issue of revision of the formula for distribution of Central assistance among States was considered in the forty-second meeting of the NDC held on 11 October 1990. At that time Sri Madhu Dandavate was Deputy Chairman of the Planning Commission and Sri Vishwanath Pratap Singh was the Prime Minister. We quote from the Summary record of discussions in the forty-second meeting of the NDC, relevant portions regarding Central assistance for State Plans:

110. Responding to the observations made by the Chief Ministers and others, Deputy Chairman, Planning Commission, Prof. Madhu Dandavate stated that they had very carefully listened to the various suggestions which had been made. One concrete result of the discussion was that none of the five alternatives was acceptable and a new or a sixth alternative had emerged and that could be called a consensus. Dy. Chairman stated that the following consensus had emerged from the deliberations:

I. From the total Central assistance, set apart funds required for externally aided schemes, as is now being done.

II. From the balance, provide reasonable amounts for only three Special Area Programmes:
(a) Hill areas; (b) Tribal areas; (c) Border areas.

III. (i) From the balance, give 30% to the Special Category States inclusive of the North-East Council.
(ii) Appoint a Committee of Experts to suggest durable solution for the financial problems of the Special Category States.
(iii) Give Assam and J&K, the same grant-loan ratio (90:10) as for the other Special Category States.

IV. Distribute the balance among the non-Special Category States as per the following formula:

Population	55%	
Per capita income	25%	(5% by Distance Method and 20% as per the existing Deviation Method)
Fiscal Management	5%	
Special Development Problems	15%	
Total	100%	

Special Development Problems will cover: (1) coastal areas, (2) special environmental issues, (3) flood and drought-prone areas, (4) exceptionally sparse or thickly populated areas, (5) special financial difficulties for achieving minimum reasonable plan size, (6) desert problems, and (7) problem of slums in urban areas.

111. Prof. Dandavate noted that there was general endorsement on other matters of detail mentioned in the agenda notes and reassured that no non-Special Category State would lose or gain more than 7% in their proportion of assistance as compared to the position under the existing formula.

115. In his concluding remarks, while referring to the Modified Gadgil Formula, the Prime Minister, Shri. V.P. Singh stated: 'We will have one round more with every State. We will not rush with it. If any State is going to face a serious problem, we will take cognizance of it. It is in a spirit of consensus and not a trick that we want to push this formula. It will be done taking into account the reasonability of every one here with mutual accommodation in the overall interest. That is the strength of this forum.'

Although Sri Dandavate stated that a consensus had emerged, immediately on conclusion of his statement, there were several interventions by the Chief Ministers. V.P. Singh, the Prime Minister, therefore, stated in his concluding speech that nothing would be rushed and that further discussions would be held with each of the Chief Ministers.

There was a change of government at the Centre in June 1991 and the Congress party came to power with P.V. Narasimha Rao as the Prime Minister. Pranab Mukherjee was the Deputy Chairman of the Planning Commission.

The forty-third meeting of the National Development Council, held on 23 and 24 December 1991, considered a number of items relating to the finalization of the Eighth Plan including 'Future of Centrally Sponsored Schemes, distribution of Central assistance and open market borrowings among States', etc.

In this meeting (forty-third) of the NDC, Pranab Mukherjee, stated that

> . . . what became known as the 'consensus formula'—did not satisfy many of the States and resentment was expressed even before the meeting ended. The then Prime Minister and the Deputy Chairman, Planning Commission, had offered to sort this out through bilateral discussions, which, however, could not take place. (Summary Record, para 14)

We have quoted above what Pranab Mukherjee had said about the 'consensus' mentioned in the forty-second meeting of the NDC. Sri Mukherjee went on to say that, 'since the issue was kept open' the Planning Commission had set up a Committee in September 1991 to examine the matter further. This Committee, according to him, felt that 'any formula now devised should remain as close as possible to the Modified Gadgil Formula because it had stood the test of time and was most likely to reconcile the largest number of expectations'. The Committee also suggested that it was necessary to provide 'incentives for good performance and disincentives for poor or non-performance in the nationally accepted thrust areas'. The Committee had proposed a formula in which population percentage would remain at 60 (as against 55 decided in the October 1990 meeting). This additional 5 per cent was to be made up by reducing the suggested 25 per cent for per capita income criterion to 20, of which 15 would be on the 'deviation method' and 5 on the 'distance method'. Sri Mukherjee justified this by saying that . . . 'even States with low per capita income might not be adversely affected by the change because even distance-wise they would be farthest from the highest per capita income and would therefore benefit' (Summary Record, para 14).

This formulation clouded the fact that the vital difference between the two factors was not the 'method' but the criterion for eligibility. Ever since the original Gadgil Formula, this particular percentage was restricted to States with per capita income below the all-India average. Now it was proposed to be thrown open to all States. This formulation came as a surprise at the meeting.*

*Personal recollections of Shri B.P.R. Vithal, the then Deputy Chairman of the Andhra Pradesh State Planning Board, who attended this meeting of the NDC along with Chief Minister, Sri Janardana Reddy.

We, therefore, reacted to this by the Chief Minister saying that 'despite several sincere efforts, the relative position of backward States had not improved and there seemed to be no justification for reducing the allocation for States with per capita income below the average from 20 to 15 per cent. However, such a reduction would not occur if the deviation method continued to apply to those States whose per capita income was below the national average, while the distance method to all States'. [sic] (para 33). The summary record is misleading here. The way it is recorded the Chief Minister was accepting the formulation presented. What he had said was that the earlier formulation (of October 1990), regarding the existing 20 per cent should continue to apply to States with per capita income below the national average, while the proposed 'distance method' may apply to an extra 5 per cent that was being allocated to this factor.

Surprisingly, few Chief Ministers objected in these clear terms to the dilution of their

Relevant portions from the Summary Record of this meeting are as follows:

309. Coming to the formula for Central assistance, which was the most important aspect of distribution of central assistance, the Deputy Chairman stated that he was happy to announce that a consensus has been arrived at on which almost all the Chief Ministers have agreed. He stated that as per the direction of the Prime Minister he had the privilege of having separate discussions with some of the Chief Ministers on the subject. The Deputy Chairman stated that the formula for distribution of Central assistance arrived at as a result of the consensus will be:

(a) Population	...	60%
(b) Per capita income	...	25%
(i) Distance method	...	5%
(ii) Deviation method	...	20%

---

original intention. On the other hand, several Chief Ministers suggested that the percentage under the 'distance method' should be progressively increased. The extreme case was of the Chief Minister, Tamil Nadu (Ms. Jayalalitha) who suggested that the entire 20 per cent might be on the 'distance method'. That night there was a discussion between Sri Pranab Mukherjee, Sri Karunakaran (Chief Minister, Kerala), and Sri Janardan Reddy (Chief Minister, Andhra Pradesh), to which I was also invited. (In his concluding remarks at the NDC, Sri Pra. .b Mukherjee said that he had had discussions with some Chief Ministers 'per the direction of the Prime Minister'.) During these discussions, I explained how, at the time of the formulation of the Gadgil Formula itself, the issue of limiting this factor to only those States whose per capita income was below the national average, had been raised by the then Chief Minister of Kerala and how his contention was finally accepted by consensus. When Smt. Indira Gandhi, as the Chairperson of the NDC, had increased the original percentage of 10 to 20 in August 1980, this criterion was not touched. It would not be correct to now change this in such a manner as to let in all the States under the guise of the 'distance method'. Sri Pranab Mukherjee was, for some reason, particular to restore the 60 per cent weightage for population as in the original Gadgil Formula. At the same time, he was keen on bringing in the 'distance method' into the per capita income factor. I suggested that this could be done by keeping 60 per cent for population but adding 5 per cent to the per capita income factor under the 'distance method' for all States, without reducing the 20 per cent under this factor on the 'deviation method' restricted to States whose per capita income was below the national average. This would mean that these States would not be loosing any thing that they had under the original Gadgil Formula but would now get an additional weightage under the 5 per cent along with all other States. Sri Karunakaran suggested that this might be accepted. Sri Pranab Mukherjee offered to find the 5 per cent from the 20 available under the 1990 formula for Fiscal Management and Special Problems. His announcement of the Revised Formula next day showed that he had found this 5 per cent by reducing Performance to 7.5 and Special Problems to 7.5

(c) Performance ... 7.5%
(The criteria for performance will be tax effort, fiscal management, achievement in certain programmes of national priority, viz., population control, elimination of illiteracy, on time completion of externally aided projects and in land reforms)

(d) Special problems ... 7.5%

310. Referring to the background of the Committee chaired by him which formulated this formula of Central assistance, Shri Mukherjee stated that even before the Committee started its work, the Prime Minister had given the direction to keep in view the need of backward States in order to see that they could improve their situation and contribute meaningfully to the development process. He hoped that the formula ultimately arrived at by general agreement would meet the need in this regard.

311. Allaying the fears felt by some States with regard to the possible errors in the computation of per capita income, the Deputy Chairman observed that the Central Statistical Organisation (CSO) will be consulted in this regard and the matter will be finalised in consultation with the States concerned which had raised doubts about the accuracy of the figures and no State would suffer on that account.

312. Referring to the criteria of performance stipulated in the consensus formula of Central assistance, the Deputy Chairman emphasised that the time had come when some credit should be given for performance. He mentioned that originally 10% was proposed but for certain reasons the percentage had to be lowered to 7.5%. He stated that the additional criterion of Land Reforms which was not originally included in the agenda and which has now been incorporated in the approved formula was as per the suggestions of the Chief ministers of West Bengal and Bihar. He stated that the Prime Minister had readily agreed to this. . . . He thanked the Council Members for giving the Planning Commission the broad support to the proposals which it placed before them for consideration.

'Performance' was a new criterion. It included 'fiscal management' which was there in October 1990. The percentages within the 7.5 for performance were later spelt out as follows.

1. Tax effort	2.5
2. Fiscal management	2.0
3. Population control	1.0
4. Female literacy	1.0

5. On time completion of externally-aided projects	0.5
6. Land reforms	0.5

The detailed methodology for all the items was indicated in D.O. Letter No. 17/3/91—FR dated 28 October 1992 from the Deputy Chairman, Planning Commission, Sri Pranab Mukherjee, addressed to all Chief Ministers (see Appendix 6.2).

EIGHTH FIVE YEAR PLAN: 1992–1997

For the Eighth Five Year Plan (1992–7) the Revised Gadgil Formula, described above, was in operation.

The thirteenth Lok Sabha, which was constituted on 16 May 1996, did not function for its full term and was dissolved on 19 March 1998. In this period three Prime Ministers changed in quick succession—Atal Behari Vajpayee, H.D. Deve Gowda, and Inder Kumar Gujral.

On 24 February 1997, Madhu Dandavate, Deputy Chairman of the Planning Commission, wrote to the Chief Ministers of States on the question of the need for further revision of the Revised Gadgil Formula and the areas of revision if the existing formula has to be revised (Appendix 6.3).

A number of Chief Ministers suggested modifications to the Revised Gadgil Formula, in response to this. In these suggestions, there was increasing emphasis on giving a higher weight to 'fiscal performance'. Exercises are on for a review of the Central assistance formula as part of the preparation of agenda items for the meeting of the Planning Commission scheduled for 27 September 2000.

With political uncertainty and frequent changes in government, nothing further has happened as regards the formula for distribution of Central assistance for State Plans. The Revised Gadgil Formula is holding fort as of now.

APPENDIX 6.1

Planning Commission

July 1990

Subject: Eighth Five Year Plan (1990–5)—Distribution of Central Budget support for State Plan expenditure: Some options for consideration.

I. *The Present Position (Gadgil Formula)*

1.1 During the first three Plans, the quantum of Central assistance for State Plans was largely decided on a schematic basis. The National Development Council (NDC) took up the question of distribution of Central assistance to the States on the basis of some objective criteria in May 1968 in the context of the formulation of the Fourth Five Year Plan. The Council set up a Committee of Chief Ministers with the then Deputy Chairman, Planning Commission (Dr. D.R. Gadgil) as Chairman to determine, among other things, the principles for distribution of Central assistance among the States for the Fourth Five Year Plan, 1969–74. The formula evolved by this Committee came to be known as the 'Gadgil Formula'.

1.2 Under the formula originally adopted in September 1968, it was agreed that:

(a) Out of the total Central assistance, a lump sum was to be set apart first for meeting the requirements of Assam, Jammu & Kashmir and Nagaland (which came to be known as 'Special Category States'; and

(b) The balance of the Central assistance was to be distributed among the remaining States in the following manner:

(i) 60% on the basis of population;
(ii) 10% on the basis of per capita income, but only to States having per capita income below the national average;
(iii) 10% on the basis of tax effort;
(iv) 10% for continuing major irrigation and power projects; and
(v) 10% for special problems of States.

1.3 The NDC which met in August 1980 to consider the Plan Frame of the Sixth Five Year Plan 1980–5, decided to modify the formula of Central assistance on the following lines:

(a) The arrangement for setting apart a lump sum amount for meeting the requirements of Central assistance for the Special Category States, as provided in the original Gadgil Formula was kept unaltered (the number of such States is ten now);

(b) The balance amount of the divisible pool of assistance to be allocated among the remaining States on the basis of the following principles:

Weights assigned (%)

	Original formula 1968	*Modified formula 1980*
(i) Population	60	60
(ii) Tax effort	10	10
(iii) Per capita income: (assistance going to States having per capita income below the national average)	10	20
(iv) Irrigation and power projects	10	–
(v) Special problems	10	10
Total	100	100

1.4 In the Seventh Plan, an amount of Rs. 29,886 crores (gross) was allocated to the States as Central assistance, which formed about 37% of the total Plan outlay of Rs. 80,698 crores approved for the State sector. The overall assistance of Rs. 29,886 crores was apportioned amongst various broad categories as indicated below:

(Rs. crores at 1984–5 prices)

I. Assistance under the Modified Gadgil Formula			
(i) Special Category States	7,102	(30%)	
(ii) Other States	16,525	(70%)	
(iii) Total	23,627	(100%)	23,627 (79.1%)
II. Assistance for externally aided projects			3,800 (12.7%)
III. Area Programmes			
(i) Hill Areas	870	(35.4%)	
(ii) Tribal Areas	756	(30.7%)	
(iii) North–Eastern Council	575	(23.4%)	
(iv) Border Area Dev. Programmes	200	(8.1%)	
(v) Other Programmes	58	(2.4%)	
Total	2,459	(100.0%)	2,459 (8.2%)
Grand Total	29,886	(100%)	

II. *Rationale for Change*

2.1 At various stages during the operation of the Gadgil Formula, there have been suggestions for modifications. However, except for the modification approved in 1980, which was obviously aimed at helping the weaker States, the core of the Formula has remained unchanged. Introduction of new factors to be given weight within the Formula, as well as alteration in the weight given to different existing factors, have been brought up from time to time. These suggestions, all of which have unquestionable merit, are often inconsistent with each other and, therefore, it has not been possible so far to evolve a new package generally acceptable to States. This is quite understandable as, in our system, all States and regions are in need of rapid economic development, though some may be relatively better off than others.

2.2 In the meeting of the National Development Council held on 18–19 June 1990, the question of revising the Gadgil Formula was again highlighted by Chief Ministers. Against this background, the Planning Commission undertook an exercise to formulate a few options for further revision of the Formula. In undertaking this exercise, the Commission was guided by two broad principles:

(1) States, which are relatively weaker in financial resources base as well as economic development, should be given special consideration in the Eighth Plan.
(2) While trying to help the relatively weaker States, too drastic a reduction in the share of Central assistance going to any of the other States should be avoided.

The Commission had informal consultations with State Governments. This consultation, done mostly at the level of Chief Ministers of a large number of States within the limited time available, gave the Commission extremely valuable feed-back on the different elements of the options available. Drawing upon this valuable insight, the Commission did a further exercise attempting to refine the available and feasible options to the optimum level of general acceptance. The result of this exercise in respect of non-special category States is described below. The components and scope of the formula that came for attention in this context were changes in the weightage or interpretation of existing elements (population, tax effort) as well as introduction of certain new elements (geographical area and social development indicators).

2.3 Before considering the principles that should now govern the distribution of Central assistance among States, one new factor emerging from the Ninth Finance Commission (NFC) report and the decisions of the Government of India thereon has to be taken note of. In its exercise to assess expenditure on the entire revenue account, the NFC assessed, what it termed, a minimum revenue Plan expenditure in the non-special category States (other than Goa). The Commission kept in view the need to correct disparities in the social and economic services in the different States while making this assessment. Based on a formula explained in the Report, the NFC recommended a total amount of Rs. 8673.62 crores as Plan deficit grants under Article 275 of the Constitution to some States. The Government have accepted this recommendation with the stipulation that it should be used as plan resource. An amount of Rs. 313.91 crores was recommended for Assam and Rs. 13.30 crores for J&K also for meeting this requirement though assessed on a different basis. These amounts (total Rs. 9000.83 crores) are being disbursed to States from 1990–1 onwards and no change in this pattern is being proposed in this paper.

2.4 Special Category States: In the Seventh Plan, these States were allocated 30% of Central block assistance. Till 1988–9, some of them got Central assistance in excess of their total plan outlays to meet their deficits in their non-plan account. From 1989-90, i.e. subsequent to the First Report of the NFC, this practice has been discontinued. Special Category States are protesting this change. For taking a view on the share of Central assistance for Special Category States, the following aspects are relevant:

(a) Most of these States are not viable fiscal units and, hence, they do have a basic handicap. Assessment made by the Planning Commission jointly with States and the Finance Ministry year after year has shown that, even after the increase in Finance Commission devolution, these States will continue to have gaps in their non-plan revenue accounts;
(b) They have, unlike non-Special Category States, no capacity to absorb their non-plan deficit through fresh borrowings;
(c) Being economically backward, they need increasing levels of plan investments;
(d) It may be noted, at the same time, that over the years these States have been receiving large amounts through Finance Commission devolution and plan transfers. A stage has been reached where some of the non-Special Category States voice the complaint that increased flows to Special Category States are adversely effecting them;
(e) The Special Category States have got used to the thinking that their financial problems would be taken care of by the Centre leading, in some cases, to inadequate concern for prudent financial management.

2.5 Taking note of these considerations, the following approach is for consideration in the context of the Eighth Plan.

(i) 30% of total Central block assistance may be set apart for Special Category States;
(ii) This will include NEC allocations also, which in the Seventh Plan, was outside this 30% and treated as part of the Special Area Programmes allocations;
(iii) Planning Commission may agree to the utilisation, by these States, of not more than 10% of Central assistance for covering their non-plan gap based on resource assessment from year to year; and
(iv) A Committee may be constituted to make a thorough study of the financial problems of these States and suggest durable solutions in a long-term perspective.

2.6 *Population*: The size of population has, by far, the highest weight among the elements that determine the share of assistance going to different States. The weight is now 60%. It is for consideration whether a small reduction (say 5 to 10%) may be made in the weight for this factor for the purpose of adding to the weight of some other factor (such as geographical area or per capita income). 1971 population will continue to be the basis for determining each State's share under the population factor.

2.7 *Per Capita Income of States*: When the original Gadgil Formula was revised, the weight of 10% for the income factor was enhanced to 20%. If the relatively weaker States have to be helped further, weight for this factor has to be increased further. Some States have pointed out that at least 30% weight should be given to this factor. Some other States have pointed out that the so-called advanced States have been suffering a steady decline in their shares of both Finance Commission and Planning Commission transfers and that it was high time to reverse this trend. The suggestion in that context from these States is to reduce the weight for income to 15% and to distribute it based on the distance from the highest income State following the methodology adopted by the Finance Commission. In determining the weight for this crucial factor, reasonable accommodation of these conflicting points of view has to be attempted. On balance, there appears to be strong ground for adding to the weight of this factor. However, with a view to moderating the impact on better-off States, the extra weight may be distributed to all the States based on the 'distance method'.

2.8 *Area*: At present, no part of the assistance under the Formula is distributed in proportion to the geographical area of States. Some States have pointed out that large areas with low density of population (e.g. Rajasthan desert) generate their own developmental problems as the investment required for creating the infrastructure for the same quantum of population is higher. It is for consideration whether we might allocate a specific weight of 5% of Central assistance on the basis of area factor. While this aspect was discussed with States, some of them pointed out that such a separate weight to area may give unintended benefit to some States for whom the problem is neither acute nor unmanageable within their own resources. In the event of the area factor not being explicitly introduced, the requirements related to large or difficult areas will need to be met as one of the special developmental problems.

2.9 *Social Indicator*: It has been argued that we should preferably look more explicitly at the quality of life enjoyed by the population as a crucial parameter of the development process and introduce it as a criterion for resource allocation. Many factors are relevant in this assessment. Literacy, primary health care, nutrition, clothing, housing, etc., would be among the prominent items in this context. Reliable State level data on all these elements are not easy to come by to measure progress from year to year or even from one Plan period to the next. Expenditure data are not appropriate for the purpose we have in mind. Even as the database is strengthened, as indeed it must be, a start could be made in the Eighth Plan using infant mortality rate (IMR) as a first proxy for the sum total of the factors that determine quality of life. If this approach is adopted, we might consider making a beginning in the Eighth Plan by setting apart a small part (say 5%) of assistance for distribution with reference to this criterion. Inter-State allocations of resources under this criterion should, in principle, focus on improvements that States bring about under IMR as measured by Sample Registration System (SRS) data of the Registrar General of India. Current data show wide variations in the IMR levels prevalent in different States. States (like Kerala) that have already achieved low IMR cannot be expected to show the same order of improvement in the coming years as States (like UP) which have a high IMR presently. One possibility would be that out of the amount to be distributed under this head, a certain percentage (say 35%) be related to base year levels of achievement and the balance to improvements on those levels from time to time.

2.10 *Tax Effort/Fiscal Management*: Presently, 10% weight is given for tax effort. Unweighted tax ratio is the basis for distribution of this part of the assistance. A State, which achieves a high level of taxation, may, by having an unusually high level of non-plan expenditure, neutralise that advantage as far as Plan is concerned. So, it seems better to replace the factor of tax effort by one covering total fiscal management. One good way to measure this might be to assess the difference between State's own total plan resources estimated at the time of finalising annual plans and their actual performance. As per this principle, those who do relatively better in comparison with their own promise would get a higher proportion of this part of assistance. To begin with, the assessment could be based on 1985–90 performance to be annually updated (on a moving quinquennial average) where data for subsequent years become available.

2.11 *Special Problems*: At present 10% of the assistance distributed under the Modified Gadgil Formula is utilised to meet special problems of States. There are, however, no guidelines regarding the type of problems for which such assistance can be given. Further, some assistance (roughly 8% in the Seventh Plan allocation) is kept outside the application of Gadgil Formula and given as special area programme assistance. It is proposed to rationalise this arrangement by (a) bringing the special area programme assistance within the scope of the formula; and (b) listing out the types of special developmental problems eligible for this part of the assistance. The weight for special developmental problems may have to be increased to 15% to accommodate the existing special area programme assistance as well as the other problems. Illustrative list could be as under:

(i) Large area with relatively low density of population, as in Rajasthan and Madhya Pradesh.

(ii) Existing special area programmes other than North-Eastern Council.

Other special developmental problems (flood/drought prone areas, urban slums, coastal areas, special environmental issues, special financial difficulties in achieving even the minimum reasonable plan size, etc.)

2.12 *Assistance for Externally Aided Projects*: In its very nature, this part of the Central assistance for State Plans does not lend itself to a distribution based on independent norms. The assistance has to be regulated according to the actual expenditure on externally aided projects. The aid, it may be pointed out, does not cover the full project cost. Further, the amount received as aid by the Centre for projects executed by States is not, as a rule, fully passed on to the States. This arrangement has, over the years, created certain difficulties for the States. States are generally hard pressed for funds to finance their plan outlays. As such, they welcome whatever additionality they can get by way of external aid. But for this purpose they have to make full provision to meet the Rupee costs of these projects. As the share of this type of assistance in the total Central assistance grows, States' counterpart funds requirement also increases. Relatively well off States manage to meet this requirement; others fall behind or struggle to attract maximum additional resources by way of external assistance by putting off expenditure on other priority programmes. It is the social development programmes that often suffer in the process. It is necessary to take note of this phenomenon in devising the arrangements for the Eighth Plan.

2.13 A connected problem relates to inter-State equity in the flow of resources from abroad. It is necessary to keep the equity consideration in view even while making the preliminary selection of projects for submission to aid agencies. In addition, the following steps would ease the difficulties faced by weaker States.

(a) In keeping with the recommendations of the Ninth Finance Commission (NFC), the entire aid meant for the projects under implementation by States may be passed on to the States;
(b) The Government of India may give advances against the likely additionality;
(c) Weaker States may be assisted to formulate projects which can be posed for external aid; and
(d) Remove any formal or informal general ban on such projects in Special Category States.

III. *Options for Consideration in the Eighth Plan*

3.1 Keeping in view the aspects brought out in the foregoing paragraphs, the following alternatives are for consideration.

Formula	*Population*	*Area*	*Per Capita Income*	*Social Indicators*	*Fiscal Management*	*Special Problems*
Existing Formula	60	–	20	–	10 (tax effort)	10
Alternative I	50	5	25	5	5	10
Alternative II	50	–	25	5	5	15
Alternative III	55	–	20	5	5	15
Alternative IV	55	–	25	–	10	10
Alternative V	55	–	20	–	10	15

3.2 As stated earlier, it is necessary to ensure that the changes proposed in the formula do not result in drastic reduction of the share of any State. To ensure this, it is proposed that if any State loses more than 7% of what it would have got under the existing formula, necessary upward adjustment will be made in its share under the new formula. This will apply only to the initial allocation of assistance for the State's Eighth Plan and not in cases where the review of the factors of fiscal performance and social indicator result in such reduction on account of State's own actual performance.

3.3 The ceiling limit of 7% will apply to increases also, in the same manner. While initially the increase will be limited to a maximum of 7%, any State's better performance in the factor of social indicator and fiscal management could earn them a higher order of increase during the annual review.

3.4 The outcome of applying the above alternatives to the actual quantum of assistance that will flow to different States has not been brought out, as the amounts due to different States under 'special problems' cannot be predetermined. Meaningful comparisons of even relative shares of total assistance that will go to different States will not be possible in view of this difficulty.

Assistance for Centrally Sponsored Schemes (CSS)

3.5 Over the years the role of CSS has increased very sharply. In the context of restoring the federal principle and paving the way for decentralisation below the State level to facilitate comprehensive area planning and implementation, the Eighth Plan Approach Paper has spelt out the need for a drastic revision in the CSS regime. Consistent with that policy, an attempt has to be made to free the major part of those funds from strict regulation by the different Central Ministries. Instead, the maximum possible decentralisation, keeping clearly the national objectives in view, has to be attempted. At the same time, reasonable checks have to be put in place to remove any apprehension that funds may be diverted from programmes of national importance.

3.6 Schemes, which are finally decided to be retained as CSS, will continue under the same arrangement as of now. Funds for the other schemes, which are to be transferred to the States, may be added to the block assistance as 85% grant and 15% loan (as most of the assistance for CSS now is given as grants). However, the utilisation of funds for schemes of national priority will need to be earmarked. It is further suggested that 5 per cent of these funds may be retained by the Central ministry concerned for giving technical and research support and for evaluation. Release of funds for these schemes will be made by the Finance Ministry as in the case of State Plan block assistance. Wherever the funds are to be spent by Local Bodies, this would also be indicated along with the criteria at the time of the transfer of funds from the Centre to the States.

Grant/Loan Pattern

3.7 In looking at possible modifications to the existing formula for grant of Central assistance, it is necessary to look also at the grant and loan components of such assistance. It has been argued by many States that an important reason for the mounting indebtedness of the States, particularly the non-Special Category States, is the 70% loan share in the assistance. The Sarkaria Commission on Centre-State Relations had also suggested alternative patterns varying from 90 (grant): 10 (loan) to 10 (grant): 90 (loan).

3.8 However, the projections of the NFC have proceeded on the basis of the existing pattern, i.e. 30 (grant): 70 (loan). It is suggested that for the Eighth Plan, the existing pattern may be retained for all non-special category States. Also, the existing 90 (grant): 10 (loan) formula may be applied for the whole (and not for parts as at present) of the assistance given to Assam and Jammu & Kashmir on par with the treatment given to all other Special Category States.

3.9 In respect of the issues raised in this Paper, Chief Ministers may like to express their views. The Planning Commission will proceed further with the preparation of the Draft Plan 1990–5 based on the broad consensus emerging from this meeting.

APPENDIX 6.2

D.O. no. 17/3/91—FR, dt. 28 October 1992 from Deputy Chairman, Planning Commission, addressed to all Chief Ministers

Dear Sri

You may recall that at the meeting of the National Development Council held on 23–4 December 1991, it was decided that in the formula for distribution of Central Assistance to the non-Special Category States the criterion of performance will have a weight of 7.5 per cent and that this criterion will include tax effort, fiscal management and achievement in certain programmes of national priority such as population control, elimination of illiteracy, on time completion of externally aided projects and Land Reforms. After taking into account the comments received from the Chief Ministers, we have evolved the following indicators in relation to the various components of the performance criterion.

1. *Tax Effort*

The basis of the criterion is the tax—SDP ratio of a State. The ratios are calculated based on the annual average tax receipts and comparable SDP of the State for the last 3 consecutive years. After computing the tax—SDP ratio, the share of each State is arrived at by converting the total of these percentages to 100. For 1993–4, data relating to 1986–9 will be used.

2. *Fiscal Management*

The criterion is based on the difference between the State's Own Resources (comprising BCR, ARM, contribution of public enterprises, small savings (excluding UTI loans), Provident Funds, Miscellaneous Capital Receipts (net), and adjustment of opening/closing balance), as provided in the financing pattern approved for the State Plan outlays and the actuals. A time period of 5 years (latest available) is taken into consideration. More precisely, the steps involved in the calculation for determining the share of each State are: (i) the difference between the State's own resources as per the Annual Plan estimate and the actual is calculated as a percentage of the Annual Plan estimate of State's own resources, (ii) the distance of each State from the lowest performance is calculated, and (iii) the share of each State is derived as a percentage of the total distances. The lowest State is also given weight equivalent to the State nearest to it. Data relating to 1987–92 (with pre-actuals of 1991–2) will be used for determining the share for 1993–4.

3.1 *Population Control*

The criterion to be adopted is the difference between the desired performance and actual performance in relation to birth rate and infant mortality rate (IMR). The desired performance rate is calculated as the difference between the goal to be achieved by AD 2000 and the actual rate of the base year divided by the remaining number of years. In this method, the difference between the desired performance rate and the actual is worked out for each State and the distance of each State from the performing State is calculated. The lowest performing State is given a value equal to the next lowest State. The States which have accomplished the goal are given the value equal to the next best performing State. These values are converted as percentages to the total to determine the share of each State in the distribution. The methodology of calculation is the same for birth rate and IMR. Since both the considerations are given equal weight, the average of the two shares is calculated for each State and this determines its share in the total distribution. For the year 1993–4, data relating to 1990 as indicated by Sample Registration System (SRS) will be used. In the subsequent years, the latest data obtained from SRS will be used.

3.2 *Elimination of Illiteracy*

The indicator in this case is the performance relating to female literacy. We have chosen female literacy, as this focuses on an important segment of the population which needs special attention. The factors taken into consideration are the female literacy rate in 1991 and the decennial growth rate of female literacy in 1981–91. In case of female literacy rate, the share of each State is determined as a proportion of each State's performance to the total of all States. A similar method is followed with respect to decennial growth rate of female literacy. Since both the considerations are given equal weight, an average of the two shares is calculated for each State and this determines its share in the total distribution. For determining the share for 1993–4, figures available from the census of 1991 will be used. For the subsequent years, some sampling system will be introduced in order to update as well as expand the information on an yearly basis.

3.3 *On-time Completion of Externally Aided Projects*

This criterion takes into account available finance in the year for externally aided projects as indicated by the Ministry of Finance in the Revised Estimates and the actual utilisation. In this method, the utilisation of external aid as a percentage of available finance for each State as indicated in the Revised Estimates for the latest year, for which information is available, is calculated. These ratios are converted as percentages to the total which give the shares of individual States. For the year 1993–4, the RE figures of Ministry of Finance for 1991–2 and the corresponding utilisation figures are the relevant data.

3.4 *Land Reforms*

The criterion for land reforms takes into account two indicators, namely, area distributed as a percentage of surplus land declared by the State and area distributed by a State as a percentage of total area distributed by all States. Both are assigned equal weights. The share of each State under each indicator is determined on the basis of each State's percentage to the total of all States. Since both the considerations are given equal weight, an average of the two shares is calculated for each State and this determines its share in the total distribution. For 1993–4, data as on January 1992 will be used.

The weights to be attached to the various components will be: Tax Effort 2.5 per cent, Fiscal Management 2 per cent, Population Control 2 per cent, Female Literacy 1 per cent, On-time Completion of Externally Aided Projects 0.5 per cent and Land Reforms 0.5 per cent. The Financial Resources Division of the Planning Commission will provide any clarifications that may be required.

With regards

Yours sincerely

Sd/-

(Pranab Mukherjee)

Criteria and Weightage under Original Gadgil Formula, Modified Gadgil Formula and Formulae as revised in October 1990 and in December 1991 for allocation of Central Assistance for State Plans

Weightage %

	Original Gadgil Formula 1969	*Modified Gadgil Formula 1980*	*NDC Revised Formula 1990*	*NDC Revised Formula 1991*
A. Special Category States	30% share for 3 States excl. NEC	30% share for 8 States excl. NEC	30 % share for 10 States excl. NEC	30% share for 10 States excl. NEC
B. Non-Special Category States				
1. Population	60.0 1971	60.0	55.0	60.0
2. On–going Major Irrigation and Power Projects	10.0	0.0	0.0	0.0
3. Per Capita Income, of which:				
(i) Acc. To Deviation Method covering only the States below the National Average.	10.0	20.0	20.0	20.0
(ii) Acc. To Distance Method covering all non-Special Category States.	0.0	0.0	5.0	5.0
4. Performance, of which:				
(a) Tax effort	10.0	10.0	0.0	2.5
(b) Fiscal Management	0.0	0.0	5.0	2.0
(c) National objectives:				
(1) Population control	0.0	0.0	0.0	1.0
(2) Female literacy	0.0	0.0	0.0	1.0
(3) On-time completion of externally aided projects:	0.0	0.0	0.0	0.5
(4) Success in land reforms:	0.0	0.0	0.0	0.5
5. Special Problems	10.0	10.0	15.0	7.5

APPENDIX 6.3

D.O Letter no. 4/9/96—FR/DCH/3670 dated 24 February 1997 from Shri Madhu Dandavate, Deputy Chairman, Planning Commission

My dear

You are aware that the normal Central assistance for State Plans has been allocated among the States on the basis of revised Gadgil Formula approved by the National Development Council in 1991. This revised formula has been adopted for the distribution of normal Central assistance in 1997–8 also.

During my discussions with the Chief Ministers for the finalisation of the Annual Plan 1997–8, some of the Chief Ministers have pointed out that the formula adopted in the Eighth Plan should be further revised. One view was that States which do relatively better in fiscal management and resource mobilisation should be suitably rewarded. An alternate view was that since developed States are able to attract more private investment, backward States should be given more consideration in Central assistance by giving higher weightage to backwardness.

A revision in the formula requires the approval of the National Development Council. In order to enable the Planning Commission to take a holistic view on the matter, I would like to have your observations, especially, on the following two points, namely whether you would like to have the formula in operation currently further revised and if so, what are the areas of revision you would like to consider. I hope that you will be able to send your considered view, on these in a couple of weeks. Based on your views and those of other Chief Ministers, we propose to prepare a note, which can be circulated among all Chief Ministers for consideration. If there is a sufficient measure of agreement on the approach to be adopted, we can consider the matter further in a subsequent meeting of the NDC.

I am enclosing a background note on Gadgil Formula for ready reference.

With regards

Yours sincerely

Sd/-

To all Chief Ministers

(Madhu Dandavate)

7

Evolution and Evaluation of the Gadgil Formula

The Gadgil Formula was evolved in the National Development Council by a consensus among the Chief Ministers of all the States. It was not as if the process by which Central plan assistance to States was being distributed before the Gadgil Formula was irrational or arbitrary. The ultimate objective of this exercise was to ensure that the size of a State's plan is related to its existing level of development and endowment. By this criterion it cannot be said that the Gadgil Formula has uniformly yielded better results. In fact, the Ninth Finance Commission in 1989 considered the lack of correlation between Central assistance and the size of the State plan as a defect in the Gadgil Formula. The grievance at that time was not based on this, but on the fact that the States had no say in the process by which Central assistance was distributed. Like, in 'No taxation without representation', the principle involved was, 'No distribution without consultation'. Representation was not expected to make taxation any more palatable; nor was consultation expected to yield any more rational or equitable distribution. Only, in both cases non-representation/non-consultation added insult to whatever injury might be inevitable in the process.

Population has the highest weightage in the Formula because, in most such exercises in our country, population has always been the most widely accepted criterion. Its primary appeal is simplicity and transparency. The population figure may be modified in some manner, such as taking into account only the 1971 census or taking the SC and ST population. But in all these modifications, there is

[*]The references to the speeches in the NDC meetings are based on my recollections. I had the good fortune of attending the meeting of the NDC in which the Gadgil Formula was adopted and the subsequent meetings when it was successively modified.— B.P.R. Vithal

the same simplicity and transparency; only the base changes. This cannot be said of the several other criteria used at one time or the other. Even the domestic product at State level took some time to gain acceptance. Such criteria may satisfy experts who understand their basis and the nature of the assumptions and approximations involved. But it is these underlying assumptions that make the criterion opaque and create suspicions that prevent a consensus.

It is generally accepted that population is a measure of the size of the task a State Government faces. Population, as a criterion, has been made more acceptable by the fact that two of our poorest States are also the most populous, viz., Uttar Pradesh and Bihar. It is not denied that even our so called prosperous States have a problem directly related to the size of their population, despite their own resources. In the National Development Council, the Chief Minister of Maharashtra once pointed out that the number of poor in his State would, perhaps, be equal to the population of Orissa or Assam. Poverty was the same, whether it was in Maharashtra or Orissa, and so how could Maharashtra be discriminated against merely because Bombay pushed up the State's gross domestic product? The then Chief Minister of Andhra Pradesh, Sri Brahmananda Reddy, said that, when the children of a rich person and of a poor person, both had fever, they deserved the same treatment depending on the nature of the fever. The child of the rich person could not be discriminated against merely because his father was rich, but the rich father could pay for the treatment of his son, whereas the poor father could not. Therefore, the poor father alone needed help in spite of the fact that both the children deserved the same attention and treatment. That, Sri Brahmananda Reddy said, was the difference between Maharashtra and Orissa. Subject to such nuances, population has been an indicator on which consensus has been easy to obtain.

The Finance Commission also gave a high weightage for population, varying between 80 and 90 per cent, for the distribution of the proceeds of income tax up to the Seventh Commission. It fell sharply to 22.5 per cent in the Eighth Commission. For the distribution of the proceeds of Union excise duties, it was 75 per cent till the Sixth Commission and fell to 25 in the next Commission. The small States, which would have had a problem by any such criterion, were kept out of the Gadgil Formula by treating them as Special Category States. The only unfortunate State that was small and also poor but got kept out of special treatment has been Orissa. This was due to its having no international border. Now, with the creation of more small and poor States, which also have no international borders, it remains to be seen how the problem of this growing number of such States will be dealt with.

Nevertheless, it was conceded that population alone could not fully capture the magnitude of the problem of development confronting each State. By the time the Gadgil Formula was being discussed, the concept of domestic product at State level was gaining general acceptance. Even if some had doubts about the methodology at that stage, it was conceded that the effect of such methodological imperfections, such as they may be, would be neutral as among different States. The Fifth Finance Commission, in February 1968, used per capita income, on the distance method, for the first time as a criterion in the formula for the distribution of the proceeds of Union excise duties, and this continued thereafter. From the Seventh Finance Commission onwards, income adjusted total population (IATP) came into use as a criterion with varying percentage weights. For the distribution of the proceeds of income tax, per capita income on the inverse and distance methods has been used since the Eighth Commission. It is against this background that we should view the weightages given to these criteria—population and per capita income—in the Gadgil Formula.

As against the declining weightage for population in the formulae of the Finance Commissions, 60 per cent for population has remained unchanged in the Gadgil Formula. This is because the Chief Ministers have not had the same confidence in any other criterion suggested to replace it. Other technical criteria, which may have looked more accurate or elegant to economists, were looked upon by the Chief Ministers as giving room for greater unspecified discretion. The discretion would later be used, not by the economists but by the Planning Commission. This is the reason that, subsequently, the Planning Commission went to great lengths to clarify to the States how the various criteria in the Revised Formula would be calculated.

Nevertheless, whatever the clarity at a given point of time, the

States were not sure how they would fare in future under such complicated criteria. Any uncertainty for the future, even if it be the result of an admittedly more rational criterion, would, they feared, give room for arbitrariness. The Finance Commissions, on the other hand, being expert bodies not continuing after their task was complete, were more concerned with greater sophistication in their criteria and not simplicity or certainty. The extreme reaction of some States to the recommendations of the Eleventh Finance Commission shows what can happen when mere technical accuracy or virtuosity is pursued without concern for the degree of disturbance in the *status quo.*

Having given a special weightage to 'backward' States, a counterweight had to be provided for 'efficient' States. The assumption that the rich were rich because they were more efficient, could be more explicitly stated where States were concerned than where classes or individuals are concerned. The Chief Minister of Punjab once gave in the NDC meeting an example of how, if a truck were given to a Punjabi, he would drive it himself and make a profit. On the other hand, if it were given to a Bihari, the owner would employ a driver and a cleaner and would soon go bankrupt. (He narrated this with apologies to Babu Jagjivan Ram, Defence Minister, who was on the dais, and who took it with a laugh.) The Chief Minister of Bihar (perhaps Sri Bhola Paswan), came up in the afternoon sessions with a report of the British times, in which it was stated that an irrigation system should be constructed in the Punjab, so that the people there, who had fought so gallantly in the British armies, could have a decent livelihood in their villages after discharge from the army. Sri Paswan said that nothing similar was done for Bihar because the Biharis were fighting the British till the end. Despite such exchanges—made in good spirit and not in mutual recrimination—it was conceded that some incentive for tax effort should be included. It may be added that, as in the case of social classes, it is not the richer States which have actually done better in tax effort, but the middle-income States. The richer States mostly derived advantage from their initial head-start.

The problem faced by States which had large natural resources for major irrigation and power projects, but inadequate financial resources, was initially solved by treating them as national projects. Subsequently, these were fitted into the State Plans. Prior to the Gadgil Formula, Central assistance for the State Plan was derived from its size initially fixed and an estimate of the State's own available financial resources. Hence, inclusion of large projects in the State Plan need not have posed a problem. After the Gadgil Formula, however, Central assistance was predetermined by the formula. The device of additionality of funds for externally-aided projects came later. Therefore, a provision in the formula became necessary for spill-over commitments on large projects already under execution. The transitional nature of this criterion is evident from the fact that, within a decade, it was given up and this 10 per cent was added for the States with per capita income below the national average.

The 10 per cent for special problems was a concession both to the inadequacy of any formula to catch all factors, and to the need to leave some area of discretion to the Planning Commission. The latter intention was brought out by the fact that, when Dr. Lakdawala was Deputy Chairman, the Commission itself gave up this discretion by stating that his 10 per cent would also be distributed in the same proportion as would have resulted from the remaining criteria.

The Formula was named after Prof. D.R. Gadgil because it was he who initiated the process and induced the evolution of a formula out of disparate interests and pressures by the force of his personality and his intellectual sharpness and integrity. The Formula cannot, therefore, be evaluated on purely technical grounds. Any technical evaluation of a formula will really involve an evaluation of the assumptions, indicators, and weightages adopted in the formula. Had this formula been evolved by Prof. Gadgil himself, as a professional economist, or by any group of economists, then their choice of various factors could have been analysed on a technical basis. The various formulae adopted by successive Finance Commissions for the horizontal distribution of the States' share of Central taxes were evolved by persons who were known to be experienced experts. Nevertheless, no less a person than Justice Rajamannar, Chairman of the Fourth Commission, described them as 'a gamble on the personal views of five persons, or a majority of them'.

The Gadgil Formula, on the other hand, was evolved on the basis of a consensus among Chief Ministers. What a consensus yields can be many things but it cannot be called a 'gamble'. A consensus may not always yield the most efficient or even the fairest result. It yields the greatest common denominator, which is accepted precisely for that reason. A consensus is like evolution. Survival is its only test of success. By that test, the Gadgil Formula has been eminently successful. Its first two modifications were merely adjustments to changed circumstances. In the third attempt a vital element of the formula, viz., the reservation of a percentage for States with per capita income below the all India average, was sought to be vitiated, but the attempt did not succeed. Thus, the basic elements of the Formula have stood the test of time and that is its greatest success.

8

Dhananjaya Ramachandra Gadgil (1901–1971) The Man and His Work

The man, whose name has been associated with a formula for distribution of Central assistance for State Plans, which has endured over the last three decades, practically sacrificed his life for the Planning Commission. He relinquished his position as Deputy Chairman of the Planning Commission on 30 April 1971 and breathed his last on 3 May 1971 while on his way back to Pune from Delhi as a result of a heart attack aboard the train. Professor D.R. Gadgil will, however, be remembered not merely because of this Formula which, indeed, formed part of his monumental contribution to Indian planning, but also for his long and distinguished record of academic achievement and public service that he had rendered before he joined the Planning Commission.

He was born on 10 April 1901 at Nasik and spent his childhood at Nagpur where his father was a Pleader. He passed the Senior Cambridge Examination and joined Cambridge University towards the end of 1918. After passing History Tripos Part I in 1920 and Economics in 1921, he submitted his thesis for M.Litt. in 1923 on 'Industrial Revolution in India'. He returned to India in July 1923, after spending five prime and formative years of his life at Cambridge.

He came from a well-to-do middle class Maharashtrain Brahmin family. His father aspired that his son should get into the Indian

* This chapter is exclusively based on:

1. V.M. Dandekar, *Dhananjaya Ramachandra Gadgil, Making of the Man*, Gokhale Institute of Politics and Economics, Poona, 1967.
2. S.A. Dange, *Professor D.R. Gadgil*, 1971.
3. Sulabha Brahme, *Professor D.R. Gadgil on Socio-economic Transformation in India*, Gokhale Institute of Politics and Economics, Poona.

Civil Service. But this was not to be. He yearned to return home and do his bit for his country and his people. He was deeply influenced by the work, teachings, and approach to life of Bal Gangadhar Tilak, who was a friend of his maternal grandfather K.B. *alias* Balasaheb Pendse. Besides Tilak, there were two other persons whom Gadgil held in great respect—Dr. B.R. Ambedkar and Bhaurao Patil.

Soon after his return to India, he accepted an appointment in the Finance Department of the Government of Bombay, which he barely held for one year (1924–5). Then began a long academic career. He was Principal of the M.T.B. College, Surat, for five years (1925–30) and then became the first Director of the Gokhale Institute of Politics and Economics, Poona, in 1930 and held it for nearly four decades. The Gokhale Institute was founded in June 1930 as the result of an endowment offered to the Servants of India Society by Rao Bahadur R.R. Kale of Satara. The Institute was named after Hon'ble Gopala Krishna Gokhale, the founder of the Servants of India Society. Thus, the Institute, as a premier social science research centre and Professor Gadgil as an outstanding research economist grew together. After retirement in March 1966, besides being the Vice-Chancellor of the University of Poona, he continued to work at the Institute as Professor Emeritus. He joined the Planning Commission as Deputy Chairman on 1 September 1967.

Professor Gadgil was a liberal in outlook and a leftist in his leanings even though he never had any political affiliations. Economic and social advancement of the oppressed and disinherited common man was his intense concern, but he aimed at achieving these objectives through cooperation and self-help rather than through coercion and compulsion. He was an agnostic who performed no rituals. But he respected the right of others to their own beliefs and never consciously hurt the feelings of others. Because of his academic stature and physical bearing, one would have felt that he was stern and unapproachable. But he was not. He was a warm and jovial person and unfailingly courteous to one and all. He was a good sportsman and a man of discipline in his habits. He was always well and neatly dressed and appreciated good food. He could attract and retain the loyalty of talented research scholars and was an inspiration to them through his own example.

Professor Gadgil's range of interests was diverse and extensive. In the course of his long, uninterrupted, and distinguished academic career of over 40 years, he filled all the positions normal to an academician and economist of his stature. The Nagpur University in 1961 and the Karnataka University in 1962 conferred on him the honorary degree of Doctor of Letters. He served on a large number of official and non-official committees with distinction. Of these, his work in connection with some more of an academic and analytical nature. The reports of all these committees bear the mark of his thought and method of approach. Professor Gadgil worked from the bottom upwards and his solutions at the macro level were based on grass roots experience. He had unrivalled experience in many areas of the Indian economy, especially in the fields of cooperation, education, agricultural development, prices and incomes policies, and multilevel planning.

His manner of conducting committee meeting was a treat to watch. His grasp of the heart of the matter, his incisive analysis of the issues, his precise language and expression, and his general conduct of the meetings, were respected by one and all. He was a faithful committee-man and insisted on having a unanimous report. In spite of his strong views on many subjects, he wished to carry others with him and was willing to compromise his known position on some issues for this purpose.

Professor Gadgil was no idle thinker. He started his career as a research economist and continued to participate throughout in movements affecting the interests of peasants and workers, agrarian problems, education, cooperative development, linguistic reorganization of State, planning, and so on. His views and solutions, at the macro-level, for various social and economic problems, emanated from his practical experience at the micro-level.

Professor Gadgil was well-known as an economist and an educationist. His writings did not draw 'notice' from political parties and revolutionary thinkers of Indian economy because, many a time, he used a very deceptive garb of abstruse terms to convey his real ideas. He was like the nineteenth and early twentieth century scientists. He was a complete economist, in the sense that his expertise was not limited to any particular branch of economics like agricultural economics, monetary economics, econometrics, etc., but it encompassed the entire spectrum of economic theory and practice. Even though the real Gadgil was hidden by the gentleness of his manner and style, his soul could not be hidden when he was forced to speak out his mind on the question of planning and reshaping of the Indian economy.

The aims of the Gokhale Institute were defined as: 'the study of and research into the various economic and political problems of India and the training of workers for such study and research'.

The objectives of social research, according to Professor Gadgil, were to understand the organization and working of social institutions and actions and reactions of people towards them, to identify the origins and drives behind social forces and the mechanism of social change and to chart out the possibilities and limitations of directing social change with the full awareness of immediate and long term implications.

He considered it important, for social scientists, to have a thorough grounding in field experience in order to deepen their understanding of the issues and enhance their grasp of the appropriate methodology. He always emphasized that the diversity of conditions and population in India called first for a local level experimentation before widening the scope of application of any programme or formulating national level policies.

From the thirties Professor Gadgil was personally involved in local level activities in diverse fields, with a view to put into practice the objectives of the Institute. Some of his earliest forays were, Survey of Fruit Marketing, Survey of Motor Bus Transportation, Survey of Farm Business, Problems of Tenancy and Rural Indebtedness, Socio-economic Survey of Poona, Problems of Lapse into Illiteracy in Satara District, etc. In all his endeavours of social and economic involvement, in-depth grass roots level investigations and analysis provided the basis for policy formulation. Empirical studies at the micro-level helped him formulate macro-level policies and planning.

Professor Gadgil was not a subject specialist but a method specialist. What distinguished him from other social scientists was his method and approach to a problem. A rigorously logical framing of the issues, an objective assessment of the available evidence, and a vigorous formulation of conclusions within a broad framework of social values and objectives marked his method. Though the method came to him naturally, he was not unaware of its importance to the proper development of social sciences. Out of his own experience and practice over the years, he organized a course in Social Science Research Method and had offered it regularly for many years to the pre-Ph.D. students in the institute.

Integration of the fractionalized Indian society, decentralization of political power, and integration and coordination of policies for socially oriented economic development, could be broadly described as the main tenets of Professor Gadgil's approach to socio-economic transformation of the Indian society. He believed that:

(a) it is only through a federation of a number of homogeneous regional communities that the basic unity and identity of the Indian society, along with all its diversities, could be truly attained;
(b) it is important that political power is systematically decentralized and areas of jurisdiction of the institutions, at various levels, are carefully delineated;
(c) there has been an increasing domination of the alliance between high-level bureaucrats, political leaders, and the economically powerful industrial and business groups. Unless this unholy nexus is broken, this alliance will continue to corner the largest share of the national income and the weaker sections of the community will get further impoverished.

For achieving this objective, he considered regional balance and development through cooperative organization as the two essential elements of economic development under Indian conditions. The regional development programme should cover exploitation of the productive assets of the region and adequate provision of infrastructure facilities—economic and social. The vehicle for achieving them should be the cooperative participation of the people of the region in all social and economic activities. He visualized the reorganization of the society to approximate a cooperative commonwealth where decentralized cooperative units would function more or less autonomously and yet in a coordinated fashion. Cooperative movement as envisaged by him was to encompass a very comprehensive field of operation in an integrated manner. Professor Gadgil considered cooperation as the only path, which will help take the economic process to the people at large and also help ensure the active participation of the people in the development process. He apprehended that unless all sections of the Indian society worked assiduously for the organization of a cooperative commonwealth for the goals set forth, the country would land itself into a situation of regional, linguistic, religious, social, and economic anarchy.

Professor Gadgil believed that the operation of the mixed economy could be so oriented as to ensure minimum standards of living to the masses, effectively curb the conspicuous consumption by the richer sections of the community, and optimum utilization of the productive resources of the community as a whole. But there are a number of conditions, which must be fulfilled for the implementation of such an integrated policy.

He emphasized the need for an integrated policy for the regulation of productive activity, credit, and prices as crucial for planned development. This implied:

(a) setting up priorities in production and curbing the monopoly power in industry and business;
(b) social control of the banking and credit structure to ensure flow of funds to priority sectors and sections according to planned programme of investment;
(c) a proper price policy; and
(d) choice of appropriate technologies—a mix of labour intensive as well as high technology methods.

Professor Gadgil had a unified system of thought on the question of development of an under-developed country. He generally described this as planning for a 'socialist society'. He believed that this would involve: 'a progressive widening of the public sector which is an essential prerequisite of any progress towards a socialist society, particularly in an underdeveloped country undertaking rapid planned development'. He also recognized the role of the private sector. There has never been any suggestion that the large field of private enterprise should be disturbed or included in the public sector. But, he wanted to restrict monopoly capitalism in the banking, insurance, large scale machine industry, mining, plantations, foreign trade, internal wholesale trade, stock exchanges, etc. He charged that 'State policy has actively helped the exploitation by the constituents of the field of modern business of their position as monopoly capitalists. As long as large private business was looked upon as a crucial medium in capital formation, its economic resources will give it the power to dictate.'

He believed that, 'mere fiscal devices will not be able to solve the problem. The only real solution to the problem, in the long run, is that the whole of this division at present occupied by monopoly capitalists should be transferred to the public sector.' Therefore, what was necessary was a 'rapid expansion of the public sector and deliberate operation of all government finance and guarantee corporations in favour of small-dispersed business as distinct from large concentrated business'.

Professor Gadgil was convinced that the existence of private monopoly capital was a hindrance to decentralization. The British policy of location of industries, trade, commerce, etc., was linked to the imperialist home market. However, even after Independence the indigenous private monopoly capital was following the same path of skewed development, leading to further enhanced unevenness of development. Professor Gadgil was for decentralization of industry and development of cooperative institutions, which alone could lead to a planned and regionally balanced social and economic infrastructure, which was essential for a reduction of inequalities.

Let us now turn to his views on agriculture. He believed that despite abolition of landlordism, the laws on land reforms and ceilings on land holdings, concentration of a major portion of land in a smaller percentage of the total number of peasant producers, continued to dominate the agricultural scene. 'In this uneven situation (of holdings) the new agricultural technology (of high yielding varieties) tends to add a further dimension of disparity between those who have the resources to make use of it and those who have not.' He was of the opinion that: 'whatever has been done in a small number of directions, it was where a fairly small number in agriculture with proportionately large resources can go ahead.' In his note on the Third Five Year Plan, he said: 'stabilisation of agricultural prices has been an accepted plank in government policies for almost a decade. Its need in underdeveloped economies has been widely accepted. In spite of all this, Government has consistently opposed and avoided in practice the adoption of a policy of stabilisation of agricultural prices.' A programme of stabilization could be undertaken through either the entry of the Government in a substantial way in trading in agricultural products or a rapid cooperativization of the field combined with certain overall operations of the Government.

Either of these courses will affect seriously the strong entrenched position of the moneylender-trader elements whose combination of the two occupations has given them a strangle hold in Indian rural economy. Historically, the present capitalistic community in India has grown primarily on the rural moneylender-trader base. Any undermining of the position of this base would inevitably spell disaster to the trading superstructure in the urban areas and may damage even urban financial capitalism, i.e. affect vitally those interests which are today politically the most powerful in the country.

Professor Gadgil treated the problem of prices, wages, incomes, and unemployment in an integrated manner, which is wholly contrary to that of the official or orthodox economics.

In India the most important prices in relation to products and services of modern and large organized business are administered, 'and Government exercises little or no control in the determination of those administered prices or in the fixation of their levels. In the area of consumer goods also, Government's inability to control extraordinary profits by traders and manufacturers has proved notorious. There is no *quid pro quo*, present or future, for liberal assistance given by Government.' Discussing the question of wages, salaries, and incomes he said: 'The whole set of values associated with democratic functioning of quasi-autonomous small group and with decentralisation of political and economic power makes it necessary that the leaders, the top executives and the administrators must have standards of consumption which do not mark them off sharply from the tiers below.'

Referring to the preaching of abstinence by the leaders he said:

> In a poor country where the leaders have constantly to preach the need for abstinence from wasteful expenditure, comparatively moderate standards of consumption for leaders may have a high moral and incentive value for society as a whole. Also, there is nothing in the Indian tradition or in the existing Indian situation to show that socially valuable or highly responsible intellectual effort has been called forth, only or chiefly, by high incentive payments.

Professor Gadgil was, however, aware that this would not be acceptable to the ruling classes. In that case he saw no reason why so much protest should arise about the wages and salaries of the working people.

> Whether the economic activity is in the private or public sector, whether it is conducted by indigenous or foreign operators, and whether emoluments received are in the nature of salaries, wages or profits, the absolute and relative weights of all incomes received out of the national pool are the concern of the Government and the Planning authority. And whether the payments are imposed, prescribed, permitted, or merely tolerated, they must be taken as part of the Plan. Therefore, whether through appropriate tax policy or through direct regulation, all salaries as well as entrepreneurial incomes must be set at appropriate levels.
>
> One of the main objectives of the rationalizing process (regarding salaries and wages) should be to see that, by the end of the Plan period (this was said in 1956), the range of differentials between the highest and the lowest scales of official payments should not be wider than obtaining in the U.K.

As regards unemployment, he located its roots in the same phenomenon of concentration of wealth in the hands of a few. No palliatives of linguistic or area reservations were going to do away with the roots of the main evil.

> The migration to towns or the problems of the educated unemployed do not constitute separate problems, but are merely two symptoms of the general malaise.
>
> In our situation the adoption, for any purpose, of a technique more capital intensive than that required for efficient production in any activity in the context of the total plan, is to take away a highly scarce factor from other activities and is an action which is not only un-social but also uneconomic.

He formulated the general policy thus:

> Our industrial development must be planned on a general small scale industry model with deliberate adoption of a large-scale and of concentration of capital only where modern production technique overwhel:ningly requires it.
>
> A contrary view is tenable only in the supposition that employment of all human resources is not an important rational objective, that the human and economic costs of unemployment and under-employment are no concern of the national plan, and capital in private hands in a poor and under-developed country does not constitute a grave national danger.

He was emphatic that: 'In the present conditions it is a decentralised, dispersed industrial sector that we have to build.' Once again he indicated, 'This has been a part of the political slogans of the last decade. But, in spite of all talk, official policy has actually led to the growth of the largest organised business and the largest metropolitan centres.'

Professor Gadgil understood that the class basis of this phenomenon was, 'The grossly disproportionate share of the national dividend is appropriated by those who wield political and economic power, and by the classes from whom the State and social leaders are drawn.' He felt that:

> The ruling section of the Congress party, as of all other political parties in India, is drawn mainly from the urban educated professional and administrative service class. To these have been added, in recent times, representatives of certain trading and financial classes who are dominant in modern business. It is the prejudices and interests of these that, consciously or unconsciously, obstruct the steps needed to bring about a real social revolution.
>
> The situation is, however, unstable. Exercise of power by big business cannot yet be open. There is need for egalitarian and socialistic slogans and some pressure for actual action in those directions. The apparently inept handling of measures such as State-trading in food-grains might thus not be so much due to incompetence as to the conscious or unconscious desire not to harm dominant interests, through effective operation of policies unwillingly accepted. The slongans have, so rfar remained confined to the relatively innocuous area of land and agriculture. But, it is not certain whether they can always be so contained.

Even the bureaucracy of recent years, has been developing close connections with organised business.

Professor Gadgil, therefore, put his faith in decentralized planning, drawing the masses into the formulation and implementation of developmental programmes, which alone, according to him, could act as 'some counter-weight to the existing overwhelming politico-economic influence of large organised business and of the top bureaucracy'.

These views of Professor Gadgil were reflected in his approach to the various Five Year Plans. As long ago as 1956, he demanded a clear decision from the National Development Council on 'vesting immediately with public interest all private corporations to which public assistance is given and their progressive incorporation in public sector'.

In 1959, in his Memorandum on the Approach to the Third Five Year Plan, he said:

> It is my contention that, in spite of all claims to the contrary, planning as such does not operate today. There are only schemes of public expenditure or of aid to private or co-operative enterprise. . . . Moreover, to the extent that official policy is active, it aggrávates the total effects by loading the dice in favour of traders and of large organised business.
>
> The problem of concentration of economic power and the monopolistic position held by some units in the private sector is another aspect that needs attention.

Outlining some of the measures, he commented that, 'A further step might be taken to orient the credit policies of financial institutions so as to prevent an undue proportion of available financial resources being diverted to large industrial houses.' However, he was pessimistic in that he felt that, 'the power of the State to regulate economic activity is less in India than in many western countries, which are said to have unplanned economies'. Therefore,

> the possible results of the present state of unpreparedness in this connection are that while taxation and public sector investment parts of the Plan will go through, the necessary efforts for building up the co-operative system and for regulating the activities, ion particular, of modern business will not be made. As a consequence, plan targets will be unevenly fulfilled; an even

more dangerous likely result is that social objectives will totally miscarry, and the efficiency of the present plan and the country's ability to plan for the future will be greatly impaired.

In November 1960 he expressed his fears that, 'in the not too distant future, there is bound to be definite confrontation of the actual possessors of the politico-economic power in the country, the large business interests, the top administrative and political groups and the political parties supported by them, with the mass of the common people'.

It was against this background that Professor Gadgil's acceptance of the responsibility of the Deputy chairmanship of the Planning Commission, in September 1967, initially caused some surprise. He was aware that there was an uphill task ahead of him and that task was as much political as economic. He was aware of the hostility with which his appointment was received in certain quarters. He was also aware that he had nothing to gain but only a reputation to loose. Nevertheless, he accepted the task out of his sense of national dedication and as a personal challenge. In this, his chief advantages were his profound knowledge of the Indian economy at all levels, his enduring faith in a system of social values and goals, and, above all, his pragmatism. He made a sharp distinction between his role as a professional critic of the Government's social and economic policies and his role as a person charged with the responsibility of actively shaping these policies. It puzzled many as to how far and how long he could maintain this distinction.

The puzzle was solved when the Prime Minister, Mrs. Indira Gandhi, asked Professor Gadgil, in April 1971, to resign and he complied. He had to go because he was too independent, too idealistic, too sincere, and too committed to the ideal of a true political and economic democracy in our country, to fit into the government mechanism. After four years as the head of the Planning Commission, he realized that he could not win the battle he had been fighting since almost the beginning of the era of planning in our country.

Professor Gadgil was ever prepared to moderate his strong views, up to a point, but not to give up his principles. The battle from outside had strengthened him but the battle from within killed him. He finally sacrificed his life for his principles, going out of the

Planning Commission and out of this world almost simultaneously. With this, the era of a patriarch, an intellectual patrician, and a social philosopher, came to an end. But he has left behind his thoughts in his profound and prophetic writings on the economy and politics of India and his stamp on a vital aspect of Centre-State relations in the country.

POSTSCRIPT

The economic paradigm that Professor Gadgil, along with many other eminent economists of his generation, accepted is no longer considered either relevant or valid. Few economists would, today, agree that the 'power to dictate' which 'large private business' acquires by its crucial role in capital formation can be curbed only by transferring this role to the public sector. Generous liberals will concede Professor Gadgil's brilliance in working out the implications and dealing with the consequences of that paradigm, such as it was. However, there are also those who will consider even this to have been a disastrous waste of intellectual talent. It is their contention that it was that paradigm that actually held up the country's economic development till it was pushed aside by them in 1991. It is not our task here to discuss the relative merits of these views. We believe that the intellectual brilliance and integrity of Professor Gadgil were such that neither time nor change of economic doctrines and fashions can diminish them. It is a curious and, perhaps, an ironic coincidence that the year in which an attempt was made to change the name of the 'Gadgil Formula', was the watershed year of 1991. Yet the formula has continued to remain the 'Gadgil Formula'—whatever its revisions or modifications. That the name has endured shows that the man's contribution has endured.

Appendix I

Resolution Constituting the Planning Commission No. I. P(C)/50, Dt. 15 March 1950

For some years past the people of India have been conscious of the importance of planned development as a means of raising the country's standard of living. This consciousness found expression in the appointment in 1938, of the National Planning Committee by the Indian National Congress. The work of the Committee was, however, interrupted by political and other developments in the beginning of the war, although much useful material has since been published. In 1944 the Government of India established a separate Department of Planning and Development and, at its instance, the Central as well as the Provincial Government prepared a number of development schemes to be undertaken after the war. Problems of planning were reviewed towards the end of 1946 by the Advisory Planning Board, which was appointed by the Interim Government of India, an important recommendation of the Board being the appointment of a Planning Commission to devote continuous attention to the whole field of development so far as the Central Government was concerned with it.

2. During the last three years the Centre as well as the Provinces have initiated schemes of development but experience has shown that progress has been hampered by the absence of adequate coordination and of sufficiently precise information about the availability of resources. With the integration of the former Indian States with the rest of the country and the emergence of new geographical and economic facts, a fresh assessment of conditions of progress has now become necessary. Moreover, inflationary pressures inherited from the war, balance of payments difficulties, the influx into India of several million persons displaced from their homes and occupations, deficiencies in the country's food supply aggravated by Partition and a succession of indifferent harvests, and the dislocation of supplies of certain essential raw materials have placed the economy under a severe strain. The need for comprehensive planning based on a careful appraisal of resources and on an objective analysis of all the relevant economic factors has become imperative. These purposes can best be achieved through an organization free from the burden of the day-to-day administration but in constant touch with the Government at the highest policy level. Accordingly, as announced by the Honourable Finance Minister in his Budget Speech on the 28 Feburary 1950, the Government of India have decided to set up a Planning Commission.

3. The Constitution of India has guaranteed certain Fundamental Rights to

the citizens of India and enunciated certain Directive Principles of State Policy, in particular, that the State shall strive to promote the welfare of the people by securing and protecting, as effectively as it may, a social order in which justice, social, economic and political, shall inform all the institutions of the national life, and shall direct its policy towards securing, among other things.

(a) that the citizens, men and women equally, have the right to an adequate means of livelihood,
(b) that the ownership and control of the material resources of the community are so distributed as best to sub-serve the common good, and
(c) that the operation of the economic system does not result in the concentration of wealth and means of production to the common detriment.

4. Having regard to these rights and in furtherence of these principles as well as the declared objective of the Government to promote a rapid rise in the standard of living of the people by efficient exploitation of the resources of the country, increasing production, and offering employment opportunities to all in the service of the community, the Planning Commission will:

(1) make an assessment of the material, capital and human resources of the country including technical personnel, and investigate the possibilities of augmenting such of these resources as are found to be deficient in relation to the nation's requirements;
(2) formulate a Plan for the most effective and balanced utilization of the country's resources;
(3) on a determination of priorities, define the stages in which the Plan should be carried out and propose the allocation of resources for the due completion of each stage;
(4) indicate the factors which are tending to retard economic development and determine the conditions which, in view of the current social and political situation, should be established for the successful execution of the Plan;
(5) determine the nature of the machinery which will be necessary for securing the successful implementation of each stage of the Plan in all its aspects;
(6) appraise, from time to time, the progress achieved in the execution of each stage of the Plan and recommend the adjustments of policy and measures that such appraisal show to be necessary; and
(7) make such interim or ancillary recommendations as appear to it to be appropriate either for facilitating the discharge of the duties assigned to it; or on a consideration of the prevailing economic programmes; or on examination of such specific problems as may be referred to it for advice by Central or State Government.

5. The Planning Commission will be composed of the following:

Chairman	:	Shri Jawahar Lal Nehru
Deputy Chairman	:	Shri Gulzarilal Nanda
Members	:	Shri V.T. Krishnamachari
		Shri Chintaman Deshmukh
		Shri G.L. Mehta
		Shri R.K. Patil
Secretary	:	Shri N.R. Pillai
Deputy Secretary	:	Shri Tarlok Singh

6. The Planning Commission will make recommendations to the Cabinet. In framing its recommendations, the Commission will act in close understanding and consultations with the Ministries of the Central Government and Governments of the States. The responsibility for taking and implementing decisions will rest with the Central and the State Governments. The Government of India feel confident that the States will give the fullest measure of help to the Commission, so as to ensure the maximum coordination in policy and unity in effort.

7. The work of the Planning Commission will affect decisively the future welfare of the people in every sphere of national life. Its success will depend on the extent to which it enlists the association and cooperation of the people at all levels. The Government of India, therefore, earnestly hope that in carrying out its task the Commission will receive the maximum support and goodwill from all interests and, in particular, from industry and labour.

8. The headquarters of the Commission will be at New Delhi.

Appendix II

Resolution Reconstructing and Redefining the Functions of the NDC

CABINET SECRETARIAT
(Department of Cabinet Affairs)
RESOLUTION
(National Development Council)
No. 65/15/CF - 67

New Delhi, 7 October 1967

The National Development Council was set up in August 1952 to strengthen and mobilize the effort and resources of the nation in support of the Five Year Plans, to support economic policies in all vital spheres and to ensure the balanced and rapid development of all parts of the country. The Council is presently composed of the Prime Minister of India, the Chief Ministers of all States and the Members of the Planning Commission, and it makes its recommendations to the Central and State Governments.

2. The Administrative Reforms Commission, in its recent Report on the Machinery of Planning, dealt with the role and functions of the National Development Council. Government have considered the recommendations of the Commission and have decided to reconstitute the National Development Council and redefine its functions.

3. The functions of the National Development Council will be:

(i) to prescribe guidelines for the formulation of the National Plan, including the assessment of resources for the Plan;
(ii) to consider the National Plan as formulated by the Planning Commission;
(iii) to consider important questions of social and economic policy affecting national development;
(iv) to review the working of the Plan from time to time and to recommend such measures as are necessary for achieving the aims and targets set out in the National Plan, including measures to secure the active participation and cooperation of the people, improve the efficiency of the administrative services, ensure the fullest development of the less advanced regions and sections of the community and, through sacrifice borne equally by all citizens, build up resources for national development.

4. The National Development Council will make its recommendations to the

Central and State Governments and will comprise the Prime Minister, all Union Cabinet Ministers, Chief Ministers of all States and Union Territories and the Members of the Planning Commission. Delhi Administration will be represented in the Council by the Lt. Governor and the Chief Executive Councillor, and the remaining Union Territories by their respective Administrators. Other Union Ministers and State Ministers may also be invited to participate in the deliberations of the Council.

5. The Council may appoint, from time to time, suitable sub-committees or panels.

6. The Council shall meet as often as may be necessary and at least twice in each year.

7. The Secretary of the Planning Commission shall act as Secretary to the National Development Council and the Planning Commission shall furnish such administrative or other assistance for the work of the Council as may be needed.

Appendix III

List of Prime Ministers of India

Name	*From*	*To*
1. Jawaharlal Nehru	15 August 1947	27 May 1964
2. Gulzari Lal Nanda	27 May 1964	9 June 1964
3. Lal Bahadur Shastri	9 June 1964	11 January 1966
4. Gulzari Lal Nanda	11 January 1966	24 January 1966
5. Indira Gandhi	24 January 1966	24 March 1977
6. Morarji Desai	24 March 1977	28 July 1979
7. Charan Singh	28 July 1979	14 January 1980
8. Indira Gandhi	14 January 1980	31 October 1984
9. Rajiv Gandhi	31 October 1984	2 December 1989
10. Vishwanath Pratap Singh	2 December 1989	7 November 1990
11. Chandra Sekhar	7 November 1990	21 June 1991
12. P.V. Narasimha Rao	21 June 1991	16 May 1996
13. Atal Behari Vajpayee	16 May 1996	1 June 1996
14. H.D. Deve Gowda	1 June 1996	21 April 1997
15. Inder Kumar Gujral	21 April 1997	19 March 1998
16. Atal Behari Vajpayee	19 March 1998	13 October 1999
17. Atal Behari Vajpayee	13 October 1999	

Appendix IV

List of Deputy Chairmen, Planning Commission

Deputy Chairman/ Minister of Planning	*From*	*To*
1. Gulazari Lal Nanda (Minister of Planning)	28 March 1950	16 February 1953
2. V.T. Krishnamachari ·	17 February 1953	21 June 1960
3. Gulzari Lal Nanda (Minister of Planning)	22 June 1960	21 September 1963
4. C.M. Trivedi (Acting)	22 September 1963	2 December 1963
5. Asoka Mehta	3 December 1963	30 January 1966
6. Asoka Mehta (Minister of Planning)	31 January 1966	30 August 1967
7. D.R. Gadgil	1 September, 1967	30 April 1971
8. C. Subramanyam (Minister of Planning)	2 May 1971	22 July 1972
9. D.P. Dhar (Minister of Planning)	23 July 1972	31 December 1974
10. P.N. Haksar	4 January 1975	31 May 1977
11. D.T. Lakdawala	1 June 1977	15 February 1980
12. M.S. Swaminathan (Acting)	16 February 1980	8 June 1980
13. N.D. Tiwari (Minister of Planning)	9 June 1980	8 August 1981
14. S.B. Chavan (Minister of Planning)	9 August 1981	19 July 1984
15. P.C. Sethi (Minister of Planning)	20 July 1984	31 October 1984
16. P.V. Narasimha Rao (Minister of Planning)	1 November 1984	14 January 1985
17. Manmohan Singh	15 January 1985	31 August 1987
18. P. Shiv Shanker	25 July 1987	29 June 1988
19. Madhav Sinh Solanki (Minister of Planning)	30 June 1988	16 August 1988
20. Rama Krishna Hegde	5 December 1989	6 July 1990

21. Madhu Dandavate (As Finance Minister)	7 July 1990	10 December 1990
22. Mohan Dharia	11 December 1990	24 June 1991
23. Pranab Mukherjee	24 June 1991	15 May 1996
24. Madhu Dandavate	1 August 1996	24 March 1998
25. Jaswant Singh	25 March 1998	4 February 1999
26. K.C. Pant	4 February 1999	Continuing

Source: Planning Commission.

Appendix V

List of Finance Ministers, Government of India

Name	From–To
1. R.K. Shanmukham Chetty	1947–9
2. John Mathai	1950–1
3. C.D. Deshmukh	1951–7
4. T.T. Krishnamachari	1957–8
5. Jawaharlal Nehru (as PM)	1958–9
6. Morarji R. Desai	1959–64
7. T.T. Krishnamachari	1964–5
8. Sachin Choudhury	1966–7
9. Morarji R. Desai (as Dy. PM)	1967–9
10. Indira Gandhi (as PM)	1969–70
11. Y.B. Chavan	1970–4
12. C. Subramaniam	1975–7
13. H.M. Patel	1977–8
14. Charan Singh (as Dy. PM)	1979
15. H.N. Bahuguna	1979
16. R. Venkatraman	1980–2
17. Pranab Mukherjee	1982–4
18. V.P. Singh	1984–6
19. Rajiv Gandhi (as PM)	1987
20. N.D. Tiwari	1987–8
21. S.B. Chavan	1988–9
22. Madhu Dandavate	1989–90
23. Yashwant Sinha	1990–1
24. Manmohan Singh	1991–5
25. P. Chidambaram	1996–8
26. Yashwant Sinha	1998–continuing

Source: Ministry of Finance, Government of India.

Appendix VI

Plan Periods and Finance Commission Periods

Plan	*Period*	*Finance Commission*	*Period*
First	1951–6	First	1952–7
Second	1956–61	Second	1957–62
Third	1961–6	Third (4 years)	1962–6
Three Annual Plans	1966–9	Fourth (3 years)	1966–9
Fourth	1969–74	Fifth	1969–74
Fifth (4 years)	1974–8	Sixth	1974–9
Two (Rolling Annual Plans)	1978–80	Seventh	1979–84
Sixth	1980–5	Eighth	1984–9
Seventh	1985–90	Ninth (1 year)	1989–90
Two Annual Plans	1990–2	Ninth	1990–5
Eighth	1992–7	Tenth	1995–2000
Ninth	1997–2002	Eleventh	2000–

Appendix VII

Gadgil Formula and its Variations

1. *Original Gadgil Formula approved by the NDC in September 1968*

(1) The requirements of Assam, Jammu & Kashmir, and Nagaland should first be met out of the total pool of Central assistance.

(2) The balance of the Central assistance should then be distributed among the remaining 14

States on the basis of the following criteria.

(i) 60 per cent on the basis of population—1965 mid-year population estimates.

(ii) 10 per cent on the basis of per capita State Domestic Product—average of three years (1962–3 to 1964–5); assistance to go to those States only whose per capita SDPs are below the national average. Deviation method to be used in distribution.

(iii) 10 per cent on the basis of tax efforts of States–State's own per capita tax receipts (1967–8) as percentage of per capita SDP (average of 1962–5).

(iv) 10 per cent on the basis of spill over into the Fourth Plan, of major continuing irrigation and power projects, each costing more than Rs. 20 crores and with expenditure of at least 10% incurred.

(v) 10 per cent for special problems of individual States.

2. *Updated Gadgil Formula (for the Fifth Plan)*

(1) Requirements of Assam, Himachal Pradesh, Jammu & Kashmir, Nagaland, Manipur, Meghalaya, Sikkim, and Tripura first to be met out of the total Central assistance.

(2) Balance to be distributed as under:

(i) 60 per cent on the basis of population—1971 population

(ii) 10 per cent on the basis of per capita SDP—average of 1970–3 to States below the average only.

(iii) 10 per cent on the basis of tax efforts of States—State's own per capita tax receipts (1973–4) as percentage of per capita SDP (average of 1970–3).

(iv) 10 per cent on the basis of continuing major irrigation and power projects.

(v) 10 per cent on the basis of special problems of individual States.

(Here, there is no change from the original Gadgil Formula. Only the data base has been updated.)

3. *Modified Gadgil Formula (for the Sixth and Seventh Plans)*

(1) Lumpsum amount to be set apart for eight Special Category States.
(2) Balance amount to be distributed among the remaining 14 states as under:
   (i) 60 per cent—1971 population
   (ii) 10 per cent—tax effort—1978–9 tax receipts and 1973–6 per capita SDP
   (iii) 20 per cent—average per capita SDP for 1973–6 to States below the average.
   (iv) 10 per cent—special problems of States.

4. *Revised Gadgil Formula (for the Eighth and Ninth Plans)*

The National Development Council, in its meeting held on 23–4 December 1991, approved a revised formula for the non-special category States as under:

(i) 60 per cent—1971 population.
(ii) 25 per cent—per capita SDP:
   (a) 20 per cent for States below the average per capita SDP—Deviation Method.
   (b) 5 per cent for all States—Distance Method.
(iii) 7.5 per cent for performance—In tax effort, fiscal management, population control, female literacy, on-time completion of externally aided projects and land reforms.
(iv) 7.5 per cent—Special problems of individual States.

Gadgil Formula and Variations

Criterion	*Original*	*Updated*	*Modified*	*Revised*
Population	60	60	60	60
Per capita SDP	10	10	20	25
Tax effort	10	10	10 (Fisc. Manage)	7.5 (performance)
Contg. Projects	10	10	Nil	Nil
Spl. Problems	10	10	10	7.5

Note: Non-special category States are: Andhra Pradesh, Bihar, Gujarat, Haryana, Karnataka, Kerala, Madhya Pradesh, Maharashtra, Orissa, Punjab, Rajasthan, Tamil Nadu, Uttar Pradesh, West Bengal, and Goa (added from May 1987).

Statement 1

Table S.1: Central Assistance to States First Five Year Plan (1951–1956)

(Rs. crores)

States	*For State Plans*		*For CSS*	*Total*
	Original	*Actual*	*Actual*	*Actual*
Andhra Pradesh	10.0	35.0	26.0	61.0
Assam	11.0	14.0	7.0	21.0
Bihar	15.0	25.0	30.0	55.0
Bombay*	22.0	42.0	38.0	80.0
Jammu & Kashmir	10.0	8.0	2.0	10.0
Kerala	7.0	13.0	11.0	24.0
Madhya Pradesh	16.0	27.0	34.0	61.0
Madras	20.0	36.0	6.0	42.0
Mysore	8.0	25.0	22.0	47.0
Orissa	10.0	11.0	66.0	77.0
Punjab	13.5	20.0	121.0	141.0
Rajasthan	9.0	15.0	45.0	60.0
Uttar Pradesh	15.0	27.0	61.0	88.0
West Bengal	26.5	34.0	79.0	113.0
Total	193.0	332.0	548.0	880.0
Gujarat*				32.0
Maharashtra*				48.0

Source: Planning Commission.

Notes: During the First Plan period, outlays on schemes such as Multipurpose River Valley Schemes, Community Development Projects, Special Minor Irrigation, Local Works, Scarcity Affected Areas, Basic and Social Education, Industrial Housing, etc., were included in the Central Sector because the exact distribution of their financial liability had not been decided upon in the beginning. On a basis comparable with subsequent State Plan outlays, they should have been in the State Sector. Figures under the column CSS represent these outlays and assistance.

* Old Bombay state was bifurcated later into Maharashtra and Gujarat states.

Statement 2

Table S.2: Central Assistance to States Second Five Year Plan (1956–1961)

(Rs. crores)

States	*Original*	*Actual (Total of Grants and Loans)*	*Grants*	*Loans*
Andhra Pradesh	100.9	96.17	19.39	76.78
Assam	33.8	30.59	14.90	15.69
Bihar	92.3	83.84	27.08	56.76
Gujarat	*	49.67	12.61	37.06
Jammu & Kashmir	24.4	19.46	3.90	15.56
Kerala	38.0	37.88	8.80	29.08
Madhya Pradesh	104.7	96.58	18.39	78.19
Maharashtra	139.3*	74.30	19.59	54.71
Mysore	73.9	67.53	14.23	53.30
Orissa	68.9	65.69	11.05	54.64
Punjab	97.1	88.29	14.23	74.06
Rajasthan	57.5	59.44	12.47	46.97
Madras	95.5	95.29	23.60	71.69
Uttar Pradesh	138.5	120.60	34.63	85.97
West Bengal	82.6	72.95	18.91	54.04
Total	1147.4	1058.28	253.78	804.50

Source: Planning Commission.
Note: * Figures are for the composite State of Bombay. Break up between Gujarat and Maharashtra are estimated for the years 1956–7 to 1959–60.

Statement 3

Table S.3: Central Assistance to States Third Five Year Plan (1961–1966)

(Rs. crores)

States	*Total*
Andhra Pradesh	220.49
Assam	99.87
Bihar	215.91
Gujarat	111.56
Jammu & Kashmir	61.55
Kerala	121.75
Madhya Pradesh	219.55
Madras	186.79
Maharashtra	166.82
Mysore	156.52
Nagaland	10.80
Orissa	136.74
Punjab	134.39
Rajasthan	161.36
Uttar Pradesh	356.24
West Bengal	155.15
Total	2515.49

Source: Planning Commission.

Statement 4

Table S.4: Central Assistance to States: Three Annual Plans (1966–1967 to 1968–1969)

(Rs. crores)

States	*1966–7*	*1967–8*	*1968–9*
Andhra Pradesh	61.25	57.50	42.80
Assam	26.40	30.00	29.40
Bihar	50.20	51.50	53.50
Gujarat	21.70	25.00	29.70
Haryana	17.00	15.00	14.41
Jammu & Kashmir	18.80	19.50	21.70
Kerala	28.30	31.00	30.40
Madhya Pradesh	43.80	49.50	48.60
Maharashtra	25.75	33.00	52.27
Mysore	36.25	36.00	36.90
Nagaland	5.11	6.25	6.00
Orissa	30.02	26.00	24.70
Punjab	20.70	16.00	15.07
Rajasthan	36.94	39.00	43.55
Tamil Nadu	40.05	38.00	42.90
Uttar Pradesh	94.32	87.50	77.60
West Bengal	31.30	34.00	47.40
Total	587.89	590.25	616.90

Source: Planning Commission.

Notes: (1) Figures represent allocations.

(2) Total assistance of Rs. 590 crores for the Annual Plan 1968–9 was distributed among individual States on the basis of the proportion between the five year assistance for individual states (1966–71) and the total assistance available to all the States, after applying a correction factor to the extent of 1/3 of over payment or short payment of assistance during 1966–7 and 1967–8, as the case may be. An additional amount of Rs. 26.90 crores was allocated later for major and minor irrigation schemes in a few States.

Statement 5

Table S.5: Central Assistance to States: Fourth Five Year Plan (1969–1974)

(Rs. crores)

States	*Allocation*	*Disbursements*
Andhra Pradesh	240.00	232.33
Assam (incl. Mizoram)	182.80	173.47
Meghalaya	37.20	30.49
Bihar	338.00	327.19
Gujarat	158.00	153.56
Haryana	78.50	76.32
Jammu & Kashmir	145.00	138.64
Karnataka	173.00	167.04
Kerala	175.00	170.10
Madhya Pradesh	262.00	253.59
Maharashtra	245.50	238.88
Nagaland	35.00	33.48
Orissa	160.00	155.43
Punjab	101.00	97.46
Rajasthan	220.00	212.69
Tamil Nadu	202.00	196.55
Uttar Pradesh	526.00	510.40
West Bengal	221.00	212.78
Total	3500.00	3380.30
Himachal Pradesh	101.40	98.44
Manipur	30.25	26.13
Tripura	34.66	29.83
Grand Total	3666.31	3534.70

Source: Planning Commission.

Statement 6

Table S.6: Central Assistance to States: Fourth Five Year Plan (1969–1974) According to the Gadgil Formula

(Rs. crores)

State	*Population 60%*	*State Income 10%*	*Tax effort 10%*	*Irri.& Power 10%*	*Special Problems 10%*	*Total 100%*
Andhra Pradesh	157.36	–	18.59	33.05	31.00	240.00
Assam						220.00*
Bihar	212.23	77.62	15.68	26.11	6.36	338.00
Gujarat	94.11	–	23.73	32.60	7.56	158.00
Haryana	35.34	–	23.77	13.11	6.28	78.50
Jammu & Kashmir						145.00*
Kerala	76.07	22.47	29.93	15.08	31.45	175.00
Madhya Pradesh	146.01	45.29	19.76	10.50	40.44	262.00
Maharashtra	178.93	–	28.46	23.14	14.97	245.50
Mysore	105.09	–	23.32	21.84	22.75	173.00
Nagaland						35.00*
Orissa	78.12	25.89	14.82	12.18	28.99	160.00
Punjab	51.71	–	26.12	19.92	3.25	101.00
Rajasthan	93.00	29.61	22.86	30.79	43.74	220.00
Tamil Nadu	145.27	–	27.40	13.54	15.79	202.00
Uttar Pradesh	327.55	109.12	16.06	51.70	21.57	526.00
West Bengal	159.21	–	19.50	6.44	35.85	221.00
Total	1860.00	310.00	310.00	310.00	310.00	310.00

Source: Planning Commission.

Note: * Rs. 400 crores were initially set apart to meet the special requirements of these three States. The balance of Rs. 3,100 crores were distributed among the remaining 14 States according to the Gadgil Formula.

Statement 7

Table S.7: Central Assistance to States Fifth Five Year Plan (1974–1978)

(Rs. crores)

States	*State Plans*	*CSS & CP*	*Total*
I. Special Category States	845.61	159.77	1005.38
II. Other States			
1. Andhra Pradesh	409.04	123.31	532.35
2. Bihar	390.63	78.18	468.81
3. Gujarat	225.02	115.38	340.40
4. Haryana	93.31	39.03	132.34
5. Karnataka	232.80	126.46	359.26
6. Kerala	201.77	64.34	266.11
7. Madhya Pradesh	296.73	130.34	427.07
8. Maharashtra	272.22	142.45	414.67
9. Orissa	239.58	71.80	311.38
10. Punjab	139.25	51.31	190.56
11. Rajasthan	261.48	101.17	362.65
12. Tamil Nadu	341.07	102.20	443.27
13. Uttar Pradesh	799.86	156.44	956.30
14. West Bengal	242.78	84.02	326.80
Total	4145.54	1386.43	5531.97
Grand Total	4191.15	1546.20	6537.35

Source: RBI Bulletins.

Statement 8

Table S.8: Central Assistance to States: Annual Plans (1978–1980)

(Rs. crores)

States	*State Plans*	*CSS & CP*	*Total*
I. Special Category States	866.20	57.65	923.85
II. Other States			
1. Andhra Pradesh	474.31	130.26	604.57
2. Bihar	469.87	143.13	613.00
3. Gujarat	176.09	74.21	250.30
4. Haryana	118.42	31.50	149.92
5. Karnataka	198.27	96.88	295.15
6. Kerala	192.50	45.82	238.32
7. Madhya Pradesh	353.34	102.62	455.96
8. Maharashtra	357.96	109.49	467.45
9. Orissa	174.22	57.64	231.86
10. Punjab	106.85	39.60	146.45
11. Rajasthan	218.46	161.76	380.22
12. Tamil Nadu	277.84	74.88	352.72
13. Uttar Pradesh	867.85	204.37	1072.22
14. West Bengal	360.74	60.50	421.24
Total	4346.72	1332.66	5679.38
Grand Total	5212.92	1390.31	6603.23

Source: RBI Bulletins.

Statement 9

Table S.9: Central Assistance to States: Sixth Five Year Plan (1980–1985)

(Rs. crores)

States	*State Plans*	*CSS & CP*	*Total*
I. Special Category States	3546.50	800.61	4347.11
II. Other States			
1. Andhra Pradesh	1268.92	573.10	1842.02
2. Bihar	1543.19	527.94	2071.13
3. Gujarat	655.96	300.23	956.19
4. Haryana	332.98	158.72	491.70
5. Karnataka	640.03	403.44	1043.47
6. Kerala	517.71	284.60	802.31
7. Madhya Pradesh	1279.55	481.45	1761.00
8. Maharashtra	1765.01	529.97	2294.98
9. Orissa	886.14	406.51	1292.65
10. Punjab	343.71	193.18	536.89
11. Rajasthan	909.12	519.39	1428.51
12. Tamil Nadu	865.09	538.35	1404.44
13. Uttar Pradesh	2494.69	1190.23	3684.92
14. West Bengal	1200.29	589.10	1789.39
Total	14702.39	6697.21	21399.60
Grand Total	18248.89	7497.82	25746.71

Source: RBI Bulletins.

Statement 10

Table S.10: Central Assistance to States: Seventh Five Year Plan (1985–1990)

(Rs. crores)

States	*State Plans*	*CSS & CP*	*Total*
I. Special Category States	9625	1952	11577
II. Other States			
1. Andhra Pradesh	1943	268	3211
2. Bihar	2829	1168	3997
3. Goa	392	32	424
4. Gujarat	1786	724	2510
5. Haryana	630	332	962
6. Karnataka	1181	872	2053
7. Kerala	1274	466	1740
8. Madhya Pradesh	2211	1197	3408
9. Maharashtra	1997	1342	3339
10. Orissa	1496	746	2242
11. Punjab	2896	323	3219
12. Rajasthan	2489	1186	3675
13. Tamil Nadu	1863	969	2832
14. Uttar Pradesh	4611	2295	6906
15. West Bengal	1506	707	2213
Total	29104	13627	42731
Grand Total	38729	15579	54308

Source: RBI Bulletins.

Statement 11

Table S.11: Central Assistance to States: Annual Plans (1990–1992)

(Rs. crores)

States	*State Plans*	*CSS & CP*	*Total*
I. Special Category States	5485	976	6461
II. Other States			
1. Andhra Pradesh	1338	878	2216
2. Bihar	1612	766	2378
3. Goa	137	22	159
4. Gujarat	633	259	892
5. Haryana	266	192	458
6. Karnataka	667	547	1214
7. Kerala	696	303	999
8. Madhya Pradesh	1399	888	2287
9. Maharashtra	1031	970	2001
10. Orissa	804	592	1396
11. Punjab	1725	194	1919
12. Rajasthan	1041	812	1853
13. Tamil Nadu	1288	634	1922
14. Uttar Pradesh	4196	1768	5964
15. West Bengal	1111	447	1558
Total	17944	9272	27216
Grand Total	23429	10248	33677

Source: RBI Bulletins.

Statement 12

Table S.12: Central Assistance to States: Eightth Five Year Plan (1992–1997)

(Rs. crores)

States	*State Plans*	*CSS & CP*	*Total*
I. Special Category States	21705	5283	26988
II. Other States			
1. Andhra Pradesh	6507	3353	9860
2. Bihar	5238	2585	7823
3. Goa	253	93	346
4. Gujarat	2926	1590	4516
5. Haryana	1310	806	2116
6. Karnataka	3052	2324	5376
7. Kerala	2606	1362	3968
8. Madhya Pradesh	4461	3582	8043
9. Maharashtra	6621	3109	9730
10. Orissa	3443	1814	5257
11. Punjab	4161	864	5025
12. Rajasthan	4209	3096	7305
13. Tamil Nadu	5548	2039	7587
14. Uttar Pradesh	16012	4542	20554
15. West Bengal	5072	1647	6719
Total	71419	32806	104225
Grand Total	93124	38089	131213

Source: RBI Bulletins.

Index